# pho
## for
## life

## A Melting Pot
## of Thoughts

AN ANTHOLOGY

# pho
## for
## life

MODEL Michelle Krusiec   HAIR STYLIST Linda Ly   MAKE-UP ARTIST Renee Lee
STYLIST Julia Tran   PHOTOGRAPHIC ASSISTANT Donald Henson   PHOTOGRAPHER Quinn Bui

*Pho for Life: A Melting Pot of Thoughts*

Published by 13 Minutes Books — A Division of Access Group Media, Inc. 11101 Condor Avenue, Fountain Valley, CA 92708

*Pho for Life: A Melting Pot of Thoughts*
Library of Congress Control Number: 2011960966
ISBN-13: 978-1467949514
ISBN-10: 1467949515

Published in the United States of America

13 Minutes Books may be purchased for educational, business, or sales promotional use. For information please write: Special Markets Department, Access Group Media, Inc. 11101 Condor Avenue, Fountain Valley, CA 92708. www.accessgroupmedia.com

While the author has made every effort to provide accurate telephone numbers and Internet addresses at the time of publication, neither the publisher nor the author assumes any responsibility for errors, or for changes that occur after publication. Further, the publisher does not have any control over and does not assume any responsibility for author or third-party websites or their content.

www.ameltingpotofthoughts.com

Book designed by Isabelle "Izzy" Kim

Limited Edition, 2011

To all of us—
for we are storytellers

# pho for life
## A Melting Pot of Thoughts

FOREWORD
*Michelle Krusiec*

INTRODUCTION
*Wendy Toliver*

COMPILATION
*Mai Xuan Bui*

thirteenminutes

"Bless this home and all who enter."

— ANONYMOUS

# Contents

# Foreword

I first began writing my solo show *Made in Taiwan* as an attempt to understand my loving but challenging relationship with my mother. Let's face it, we all love our family and it would be unnatural if they didn't drive us…a little bit…just a little bit crazy. *Made in Taiwan* was inspired by my own adolescence and while it was specific to me, I found that hundreds of audience goers, night after night, genuinely connected to the theme of a young woman discovering her right to have a voice. In the story, the daughter learns that to command the respect of her overprotective mother, she must literally stand up and speak up for herself. It's a courageous lesson in self worth. In performing the piece, I learned as much from the show as I did from the audiences who often told me they were able to connect to my story because they felt some part of themselves reflected up on that stage. My solo show was developed, much like this book, as a collection of funny anecdotal stories intended to be humorous and entertaining, but the more I wrote, the more I uncovered my own vulnerabilities and that's when you know people start to sit up a little straighter in their seats. When people hear the truth, they pay attention.

In January 2011, I started working with a nonprofit organization called Center for the Pacific Asian Family with the intention of helping survivors of domestic violence and sexual assault heal by telling their own stories. During my training, I met a woman named Ruth Beaglehole who specializes in non-violent parenting methods and who founded Echo Parenting. Ruth said something I found absolutely remarkable and I realized was the very thing that acting had always taught me. Ruth explained that a child who is able to provide or give narrative to his or her own experience is a healthy child. Healthy children can articulate and give voice to what they may be feeling, thereby expressing their needs. We are happiest when we can express our needs and have our needs met. She shows children how to do this by encouraging them to draw and depict what they may be feeling.

This is fundamental storytelling. This is how I connect to audiences as an actor and a writer and this is how we connect to each other. We're all walking stories waiting to be witnessed and discovered.

I first met Mai and Quinn Bui in 2006 shooting the February cover of *Thirteen Minutes*. I was impressed and delighted by their enthusiasm, generosity and dedication to exploring positive images and stories of the Asian American community. They also wanted to feed me and that counts as a friend for life in my book. For as long as I've known them, I've marveled at how heartfelt and steadfast they've remained in their endeavors. I'm not surprised our reunion is through this diverse collection of living stories called Pho for Life. After all, our first lunch together was over a bowl of hot, delicious, steaming pho. Comfort food for long lasting friendships.

The stories you'll find within come from people who reflect the various complex, funny, enlightening and extraordinary every day events that all of us encounter. It's an anthology composed of our diverse community that connects every single one of us in our collective desire to create narrative and find commonality. This book celebrates the natural gift we are given as children to tell stories as a means of providing insight to both you and me. I hope you enjoy the food for thought and will find a deeper connection to these stories by, maybe, one day sharing your own.

— *Michelle Krusiec*

# Introduction

When I was a student at Colorado State University, I had to juggle several jobs to pay my tuition and living expenses. I delivered newspapers at the crack of dawn, worked the cash register at the local Wendy's (and yes, I got all kinds of grief thanks to my name and reddish hair), served cocktails to country clubbers, and performed singing telegrams à la Marilyn Monroe. Needless to say, funds were tight and like the proverbial college student, I gobbled my fair share of cereal, crackers, and pizza. Whenever I'd collected enough money in my out-to-eat jar, I inevitably found myself racing through the door of Saigon 17, a charming Vietnamese restaurant in Old Town, Fort Collins.

Growing up, I don't think I ever tried Vietnamese cuisine; it was my own little discovery. Saigon 17 and its jewel-toned décor, tiny kitchen, and smiley servers was my personal paradise where I could savor the fresh spring rolls, slurp the steaming pho, sip creamy coffee, and forget about my problems for a little while. It's also where I fell for the Vietnamese food-loving tennis player who'd become my husband four short years later. Today, when we stroll through Old Town, we stop where our favorite restaurant used to be, wishing it was still there so we could rekindle those early romantic feelings over oversized bowls of pho. Though we're sad Saigon 17 is gone, we're eternally grateful for the memories.

Food can be much more than sustenance for our bodies. Sometimes, a specific dish or meal will connect you with memories or inspire you to make new ones. It can feed not only your body, but your soul. This is why I can't think of a more fitting title for the treasure you hold in your hands than *Pho for Life: A Melting Pot of Thoughts*.

Those who've experienced it know; pho is no ordinary beef noodle soup. It's a marriage of flavors, textures and aromas that culminate in a gastronomic masterpiece. Vietnamese call it a "taste of home," and people from anywhere on the globe can appreciate pho's power of bringing together friends and family.

When Mai Bui asked if I'd be interested in lending an editorial hand to this anthology, I felt deeply honored. I knew publishing a collection of inspirational tales was a dream of his, and I wanted to be a part of that dream. Little did I know what an impact these fifty-eight stories would have on me. I shed tears when I read about the challenges facing immigrants on pirate-infested waters and laughed out loud while reading about how American TV commercials might not be the best tutorial on Eggo waffles. With *Pho for Life* stories fresh in my mind, I found myself picking up the phone to call my mom just to say "I love you," baking banana bread for my neighbor with breast cancer, and snuggling in a cozy blanket, warm from head to toe with musings of love. I have no doubt the nuggets of wisdom, confessions, perspectives, and histories within these pages will feed your soul.

You'll soon discover that the authors featured in this beautiful book represent a variety of ages and backgrounds, yet they all have something in common. They are living life as though it's a journey, taking time out of their busy careers, social circles, and family lives to dig deep within their hearts for the treasures buried there. Sometimes reconnecting with your true self means branching out and following your dreams, even if the path is rocky, steep, and dark. Other times it means coming back home—seeking forgiveness, reviving, and building upon relationships with those who love you most of all. But however difficult and diverse our journeys, we can all appreciate and learn from each other, and in result, enhance our own lives.

If you are taking this journey as well, you are part of the *Pho for Life* family. We invite you to savor each and every story as if it's a steaming bowl of pho—or whatever dish you've come to love for its ability to nourish your soul. *Bon Appétit!*

— *Wendy Toliver*

# A Bowl of Pho
## Vietnam's treasured beef noodle soup that brings families together

We're a feisty group, the Vietnamese. Get us together in a room and we'll debate endlessly over the north and south of our politics, the clashes of our history, the contradictions of our culture.

But mention pho (pronounced *fuh*) — our beloved beef noodle soup — and immediately our differences vanish. Our eyes shine, our faces beam. All of a sudden we've become an agreeable family with a love for one another that's as strong, compelling and reassuring as the beefy steam that billows and curls from a bowl of pho.

Sound overstated? Not one bit. Not if you're Vietnamese and born in the old country. For to us, pho is life, love and all things that matter. We treasure pho, and most of us have loved it since the day we were old enough to hold a pair of chopsticks. For me, the fascination began when I was five. Every weekend, my parents would take me and my siblings to Pho 79, a small, dark and run-down noodle shop in Saigon with wobbly tables and squeaky stools. Yet every time we went, it was always packed and difficult to find a table.

So we resorted to a practiced routine. With hawk eyes, we'd scan the room, searching for a party about to leave. As soon as we found one, we quickly dashed over, sort of inconspicuously standing on the side, waiting for the right moment to seize our table.

Once seated, my parents placed our usual order: *pho tai chin* or pho with both rare and cooked beef for everyone, and, for the adults, ca phe sua da — a delicious coffee drink served with condensed milk and ice.

Moments later, the server, step by careful step, slowly approached with large bowls filled to the brim. As soon as they were placed before us, a warm, thick, wavy steam arose and embraced our faces.

Bending down, we slowly inhaled the aroma as if to verify its authenticity. Yes, the broth smelled utterly beefy, laced with just-roasted ginger, anise and freshly chopped onions and cilantro. The rice noodles looked velvety and fresh, the edges of the rare beef curled up expectantly in the hot broth.

All was well.

Then, arms and hands crisscrossing, we reached for a piece of lime to squeeze into the broth, a handful of cool, crisp bean sprouts, a few sprigs of Asian basil and saw-leaf herbs and fresh chiles. Against the noisy laughter and chitchat, we savored our soup, chewing, slurping and giggling until the last drop.

Even though my family first discovered pho in Saigon in the late 1950s, it actually originated in the north in Hanoi around the turn of the century.

Based on literary accounts, the cooking and enjoyment of pho surfaced sometime after the French occupation of Hanoi in the mid-1880s. The Vietnamese, who valued cows and buffaloes as indispensable beasts of burden, ate little red meat, preferring pork, chicken and seafood. But with the French affection for bifteck and dishes with boeuf, red meat began to appear in markets and restaurants, thereby slowly influencing the local diet, especially that of the upper class.

How did the increasing popularity of beef prompt the creation of pho?

It's a steamy debate, even to this day. However, some Hanoi cultural experts with ancestors who are said to have witnessed the birth of pho believe this dish parallels the history of Vietnam, harboring both a Chinese and French connection. (The former occupied Vietnam for 1,000 years and the latter almost 100 years.)

Some theorize it was the French who triggered pho, popularizing the use of bones and lesser cuts of beef to make broth. After all, in a society that wasted nothing, what was one to do with all the bones carved from biftecks? In fact, they believe perhaps it was first created when Vietnamese cooks learned to make pot au feu for their French masters. The name pho, they suspect, might have even come from feu. But others argue that while the French can take credit for popularizing beef, it was actually the Chinese who inspired the dish with ingredients like noodles, ginger and anise. Then there are still others who claim it was the Chinese, and the Chinese alone, who instigated this culinary wonder.

But regardless of the origin, Chinese or French or both, once at the stove, the Vietnamese were quick to interject their own ideas. They concocted an exciting dish, using ingredients inspired by their foreign rulers but customizing it to include nuoc mam, or fish sauce, the defining characteristic of the local cuisine.

In the 1930s, in part spurred by nationalistic sentiments, some Hanoi scholars wrote passionately about pho, a food that not only cleverly provided all the necessary nourishment in one convenient bowl, but one that also symbolically freed the Vietnamese. At last, the Vietnamese succeeded in their fight for self-determination; finally they were free to express themselves, if only through their pho.

Huu Ngoc, a prolific author and cultural expert who's written that pho is a contribution to human happiness, recently recalled his memories of those times: "Pho was very special, almost status food. We loved it because it had everything we valued — rice noodles, broth, meat and vegetables. It was complete, nutritious, infinitely delicious and yet so easy to digest that we could eat it morning and night, day after day."

In 1954, the infectious enthusiasm and following for this dish spread South. Vietnam had been partitioned, and the North fell under Communist control. Almost one million Northerners fled South, taking with them a dream of a new life.

For some, this new life meant the re-creation of a pho culture.

Pho took the South by storm. My mother, a Southerner who had just moved from her village to Saigon where my dad got his first job out of military school, had never seen or heard of pho until then.

Though there were sightings as early as the late 1940s, it didn't become popular until after the mass migration of 1954.

At the time my mother and her contemporaries slurped on hu tieu, a Chinese-style rice noodle soup made with pork bones and pork meat. "When I first tasted the pho, I thought it was incredible," my mother remembers. "It was similar to hu tieu, but the aromatic beef stock and and roasted spices made it so much more exciting. I knew instantly it was the soup to eat."

From then on, whenever she and my father could afford it, which was about once a month, they would treat themselves to this new delicacy.

In the South, pho became highly embellished. Reflecting the abundance of its new surroundings, it had more meat (imagine the portion now in the United States), more noodles, more broth. Because Southerners are by nature indulgent — demanding richer, livelier flavors and textures — bean sprouts and rau thom or fragrant herbs such as saw- leaf and basil were added.

And it didn't stop there. Garnishes such as lime wedges, fresh chiles, chile sauce and tuong, or black bean sauce, were served alongside, giving the soup a dimension never before experienced. As in the north, it quickly became a favorite, but only after it had been modified to fit and reflect southern taste.

In 1975, when my family first arrived in the United States after the fall of Saigon, we desperately missed pho. At the time there weren't many noodle shops. But when we did find one, the soup usually didn't taste that good because of the lack of Asian ingredients, particularly herbs. Yet we ate it whenever we could, great or not. To us a steaming bowl of pho was a welcoming thought. A taste of home, it warmed our spirits and gave us the comfort and solace needed in our first difficult years.

Fortunately, over time, immigrant families such as ours have successfully readjusted to our new life in America. And somehow, in the midst of all this transformation, pho — which followed us through tumultuous times and journeys — also became integrated into our present- day life. Authentic recipes have been dusted off, preserved and executed with great fervor.

Noodle shops have now proliferated throughout the United States, opening not only in the traditional enclaves of immigrant communities, but in mainstream neighborhoods as well. In many shops, Asians and Westerners sit side by side, munching on the long, chewy noodles. The appeal of this soup — once felt only by native connoisseurs — has spread beyond nationality and attracted a new following. As before, pho has once again survived and triumphed.

For me, even decades after my childhood days in Saigon and thousands of miles away from my native country, pho remains my obsession. If I'm not eating a bowl of pho, it lurks in my consciousness, its enticing aromas assuring me that, somehow, it will always be a part of my life.

*Mai Pham is the owner of Lemon Grass and Star Ginger*
*Restaurants in Sacramento, California*

> "Some people say they haven't yet found themselves. But the self is not something one finds; it is something one creates."
>
> THOMAS SZASZ

# I Became American and the World Kept Turning

When I was seventeen, I became an American citizen. The woman from Immigration Services sat across a broad desk and asked me to name the third President. When I did so swiftly — after all, my high school was named after him — in a standard American accent she seemed surprised and said, "Oh, you're an American." Well, not technically.

Instead of asking me more questions — my mom had been posed three, including, "What was the main reason over which the Civil War was fought?"— she pulled out a piece of paper and told me to sign it. It began, "I hereby declare, on oath, that I absolutely and entirely renounce and abjure all allegiance and fidelity to any foreign prince, potentate, state, or sovereignty of whom or which I have heretofore been a subject or citizen…" As you might imagine, this was a lot to take in for a seventeen year old. What exactly was being asked of me here? I knew I was technically a foreigner, and, if we're being really technical, a subject of the People's Republic of China, but did I have any allegiance and fidelity to that country? It was an ocean away and I hadn't visited in years. I looked at my Chinese passport. I had never liked its shade of burgundy but now, faced with having to relinquish it, I felt a pang of distress that I had not cherished it more.

I signed the paper. The woman took my passport — or had I handed it to her, like Abraham offering up Isaac? — and put it in her drawer and that was it: I was an American.

I waited for a sign — a chorus of angels, a burst of light — but there was nothing. I was still me, and the world kept quietly turning. My mother picked up her purse and we drove home. Two weeks later I received a new passport in the mail. It was navy blue and I couldn't help thinking that I liked this color better than that rusted burgundy.

Five years later, after college, I came back to China on a lark. I wanted, as in an old bildungsroman, to find out who I was. But I quickly discovered that my identity confused people. A common conversation went like this:

"Are you a Chinese?"

Well, I was born in China and moved to America when I was very young.

"So you're an ABC."

Not quite. ABC stands for "American-born Chinese" and, as I just explained, I was born in China, so I guess, if you had to, you could call me a CBA, a "Chinese-born American."

"So you're an American?"

That depends on what you mean by "American." I have an American passport.

"You talk like an American."

Well I have lived there for nearly two decades.

"So you're Chinese-American."

I guess you could say that.

"But you look Chinese."

Because I am ethnically Chinese.

"So that makes you Chinese."

Right.

It was frustrating at first, having people cram me into whatever racial box suited them. I was Chinese so long as they liked me, but if I made a comment critical of China or not in line with "traditional Chinese thinking," they would counter with the pseudo-rhetorical:

"你是中国人吗?", "Are you Chinese?"

I never knew how to answer that. I can't blame people for wanting simple answers to complex questions. Chinese people, coming from a largely homogenous society, are used to thinking about race in black-and-white and, because the culture discourages individuality, often conflate the concepts of nationality, race, and identity.

My nationality is American and I am a member of the Han race. But the question of identity is much trickier. I am a product of two cultures, as trite as it sounds—which is to say that I am influenced by two ways of thinking more or less equally. I was raised in a Chinese household but spent most of my day in American society.

This caused problems. When I was growing up, my parents made me go to Chinese school every Sunday from 2 to 4 p.m. in order to learn Mandarin and retain some semblance of being Chinese. I went for ten years. Today, I'm thankful for being able to speak Mandarin as it has helped my work and life in Beijing immensely. But growing up, I tried to get out of it every week. I didn't understand why my friends got to sleep over on Saturdays and didn't have to learn another language on the Sabbath.

I think Chinese school, more than anything else in my childhood— more than the dismissive way girls looked at me, more than my lack of musculature or the size of my family's apartment compared to my friends' houses–contributed to my sense of not belonging, my sense that I was different, not in a cheesy, unique snowflake kind of way, but that something deep down separated me, irrevocably, from others, and from America.

So when I came to China after college, I tried to see if I could belong here. I decided to do my best to blend in. If I didn't talk too much, no one should be able to tell me apart—I'd just be another bespectacled Chinese man. And yet this failed spectacularly. After being in Beijing a month, I walked up to the counter of a Dairy Queen and ordered a Blizzard. The girl at the counter asked, "You're not from this country, are you?" I ask her how she could tell. "I don't know," she said. "Something about your 气质 (disposition), the way you walk." How strange, I thought, after all that posturing, my stride had given me away.

In retrospect, it was foolish of me to think I could belong to a country I had no memories of and had only visited sporadically. But it made me wonder: was there really no place in the world I could call myself a part of? It's a question I sometimes ponder in the moments when my mind idles before sleep. Did I ever have a choice in who I've become? Could any child born in China, brought to the United States at the age of four, and raised there under the strict supervision of Chinese parents, be any different? Then, if sleep still hasn't taken me, I do a little thought experiment: I tweak the variables of my early childhood and construct my life in that alternate reality. What if I had gone to the United States as a teenager? What if I had been born in America? Who would I be then?

Imagining life in these bizarro worlds makes for somnolent fun but I inevitably arrive at the same conclusion: who I could have been is nowhere near as interesting as who I am now. There's no one else, and no place else, I'd rather be. Sure, I sometimes feel isolated, misunderstood, and alone, but those emotions are present in every life, not just those of immigrants or minorities.

If anything, my upbringing has made me look for something more than race and nationality by which to define myself. It has made me restless and inquisitive. My want for a sense of belonging made me go out into the world. My failure to find it compelled me to stay there. Most of all, my experiences have made me see that petty human distinctions such as race and nationality, not to mention gender and sexuality, don't mean anything beyond the physical, beyond boxes on a form and the hue of a passport. They don't determine anything when it comes to your life and they fall far short in defining who you are. Your identity, like your future, is something you construct for yourself. That's why there were no angels or bursts of light. I was still me, and the world kept quietly turning.

"A friend's writing on an envelope lifts the heart on the rainiest morning."

CHARLOTTE GRAY

letters from overseas

*to Otto Wirgau*

you say, *it's the rainy season and we are finally getting our share*

the small mountains crop up like thorny
ridges on the back of a dragon, visible for hundreds of miles

people buried in mudslides

it seems Sung Yat-sen's birthplace was a typical village

the dragon is made up of eight different animals

you say, *last year it rained for twenty-two days straight*

you are writing during the five hour boat trip down the Li River

you say, *the body is a gift*

*I am a list of questions that can't be confined*

we have had so much rain that our phones have been malfunctioning

do I mail you a copy of the article about the boy
who almost jumped off the cliff?

you say, *it was nice to sit by the River Li*

we are on Tai Tam Road again during the Gulf War
and the bomb threats have driven us to the beach

you ask, *is pride a positive or negative force?*

the junk sways on Repulse Bay

I say, *the search is over*
you ask, *does there have to be a god?*

I say, *you write me a four line paragraph and I write you a book* you say, *my eyes begin to burn*

no, I don't know where those midwestern states are located

you say, *a little geography is good for you*

on the other side of town twenty people were trampled to death

we tried the black market for plane tickets

disembarked at Yangshuo

the boy sat next to his dead body until they took him away

you say, *it was obvious that his torso had been removed*

we watched the *Sound of Music* on an old VCR

the TV was shooting sparks and smoke

there were no fire extinguishers

some saw his body on the ground

he made his name out of styrofoam and the letters
floated down the pond

I say, *he is leaving for school next month*

you say, *it has taken a number of days to function again*

this weekend is the Queen's birthday

you say, *yes, we must see each other*

if I was within hearing range, it would have sounded like C natural

"A man in love is incomplete until he is married. Then he's finished."

ZSA ZSA GABOR

# Marrying Japanese

When I was single, I asked my mother to set me up with one of her friend's daughters. Every year, I've seen Christmas pictures of these beautiful girls in All-American families. I've watched them grow into legally datable women from presumably mother-approved families. I told my mother my preferences: Preferably hot. Preferably cool. Preferably smart.

A few days later, Mom presented me with the name of a Japanese American woman a couple years younger than me. I asked her if the woman was beautiful, she admitted that the girl was chubby. I asked her if this young lady was smart, she told me that wives didn't need to be intelligent. Exasperated, I asked if she at least had a nice personality. My mother's response was that she would make a great wife.

I ended up meeting her anyway.

This is of course the same mother who has given me a preference list on which races I should and could marry. First on that illustrious list is Japanese. Since my mother is Japanese, she wants to make sure she has someone to speak to when she's old and forgets English. Next is Caucasian, because according to her if my wife isn't Japanese (what a disappointment I would be), the best she can hope for is beautiful grandchildren. Chinese is third. She prefers a wealthy woman from

Taiwan or Hong Kong to those from the Mainland. After that, it's a slippery slope she doesn't like to discuss.

Mom has admitted in the past that if I were to date outside the first three choices, she would accept my future life partner as long as I was happy. But she says this with such a grudging acceptance, I know she would be disappointed with my bad judgment. In other words, unless I was really in love and willing to put in the time and effort needed to ensure my mother's contentment, I shouldn't bother.

She has nothing to worry about, though. Asian men are not seen as desirable. I read a poll in college that surveyed the general perceptions of racial beauty in America. For women, Asians were seen as the most beautiful, followed by Caucasians, Latinas, and then African Americans. For males, that list was flipped around. African Americans were ranked number one, Caucasians were next, then Latinos, and finally Asians. Most of the comments were based on stereotypes. Those surveyed said that Asian men were feminine, small, computer geeks or martial arts experts, untrustworthy, perverted, and sneaky.

With so many pre- and misconceptions of me, it's little wonder that I've only dated twice outside my race. Both were white women with histories of dating other Asian men. This is known as "yellow fever."

It's rare to see Asian males with non-Asian females. The opposite isn't as true. Everywhere I go, I find Asian women with men from every other race. I'm not mad at them, but I just think it's funny how fashionable it's become to have an Oriental doll hanging from the arm. Even Harry Potter had a crush on an Asian classmate!

Gay Asians typically don't date other gay Asians. How messed up is that? If I were homosexual, I'd marry an Asian man. That's called "sticky rice."

But instead, we've always been regulated to the role of the friend who is so nice and so loyal and so friendly and so respectable. A sucker. Just once, I want to hear about a blond-haired, blue-eyed model who went out with an Asian guy strictly for his looks.

In the end, my mom's ultimate wish came true. I married a woman of Japanese descent who speaks Japanese fluently and who I happen to love more than anyone else I've ever met. It's nice when it works out for everyone. You're welcome, Mom.

# No Ordinary Lunch

I hoped no one was watching as I opened up my red lunch box. Slowly, just a crack. Objects obscured in shadow peeped back at me like a triad of spies. I closed the lid, and looked around as my fellow eight year-old classmates rummaged into their own brown bags or plastic lunch boxes so similar to mine. A dark haired boy took out a plastic sandwich bag, exposing a perfect square of white bread, crusts neatly cut off. A girl who always shared her graham crackers sat next to him biting into her own half of a peanut butter and jelly sandwich. With crusts. This was your average lunch hour, average school cafeteria, filled with average grade schoolers. What wasn't so average was my lunch.

This was third grade in the eighties. And as far as my memory could reach, I've always felt self-conscious about the food my mom packed for me. My family was the typical of immigrants: middle-class Korean parents who migrated from a spit of a peninsula to the vast United States, leaving the old behind to cultivate their dreams for something better. And much to my callow dismay, the food culture of our Mother Country fell into the "take with us" pile. For a kid just trying to fit in, this was dystopia.

Unlike the moms of my classmates who stocked their fridge and pantries with the same delicious processed deli meats and covetous sugary snacks, my own mother seemed oblivious to these typical American food choices. Instead, sticky white rice wrapped in a sheet of dry seaweed stuffed with pickled radish, cucumbers, and imitation crab meat (aka: *kimbap*); or a mound of rice topped with a fried egg (fried in sesame oil nonetheless) with a side of sweet-and-spicy baby anchovies; and the exotic like, were more likely to make an appearance once I lifted the plastic lid. So while the other kids swapped or gleefully chomped on their Oscar Mayer bologna sandwiches and Little Debbie snack cakes, I was left to face my alien lunch alone.

But what my mother lacked in knowledge on bagged lunches, she made up for in her Korean cuisines with culinary exactitude and impeccable attention. If there is any group of people who has an uncanny knack for quantitative, left-brained activities, I'd say Asians would have Olympic qualifications. Look at the stereotypes: from nerdy tutors to badass ninjas—all attest to this with a sort of penchant for precision and discipline. And this aptitude also ran deep in my mother's own heart. Aside from the fact that my lunch meals were, as some kids would bluntly point out, "funny smelling" and "weird," the food the dear woman prepared were aesthetic and thoughtful. Maybe it's because she grew up during a time and place, where traditionally, as a daughter, she was expected to take on kitchen duties; to feed and nurture the family while her older brothers attended school. If she made *kimbap*, each roll was sliced without a variation in its circumference size and width, as if she held a mental ruler as a grid. Even each respective vegetable was sliced and cubed and scaled to mirror each other, to lay perfectly side by side in a burrito of rice and seaweed. And even 8000 miles from Korea, she held on to her cultural upbringing and the understanding that cooking for your family can be more than just a chore; it becomes a thought for the interest of others. It's no wonder she never packed an ordinary lunch. I realize now that no mother does. It's an expression of their extraordinary love.

Time and my emphatic wheedling eventually led my mother to attempt to emulate the American packed lunch. It took a few attempts though. As if to compensate for its less immaculate nature, she couldn't help herself from making them just a little bit different; I was the only kid who brought ham and cucumber sandwiches. On toasted bread.

Back in the noisy cafeteria, I determinedly opened my beautifully mundane lunch box and took out the contents one by one: a thermos, a pair of plastic pink chopsticks, and a shallow, square container whose clear lid exposed perfect squares of fried tofu stacked neatly alongside a huddle of baby potatoes stewed in soy sauce. And rice. Alas, who can doubt a mother's love.

"All that I am, or hope to be,
I owe to my angel mother."

ABRAHAM LINCOLN

# A Mother's Love Cuts Wide, Straight & Deep

The announcement for a lunch break had barely started, but I was already out of the jury assembly room. I did not want to be late on my lunch date with the most beautiful woman on earth. I love and adore her. My family cherishes her. An hour and thirty minutes with someone I had the utmost admiration for would not be long enough. I needed to get going.

It was a perfect day in May. The sky was blue, sun bright. A cool breeze caressed the colorful flowers along the street.

But on this spectacular spring day, the only thing I saw was the emptiness inside me. The only thing I felt was a deep sense of helplessness and hopelessness.

As I hurried along, nothing seemed to move.

"Come on, I don't have all day," I mumbled impatiently, as though others could hear it.

The television was on but she was asleep when I entered the room. Next to her, sitting on a lunch tray, was a dish of melted ice cream.

I stood there until she awoke. Glittered with joy and love, she tried to sit up, but the tubes connected to her body were in the way.

"I'm glad to see you!" said the woman. "I was worried that they would take away your favorite dessert before you could get here."

Mom had been in the hospital for two days now. Although she looked well and could not have been more alert, the doctors did not have good news. According to their predictions, my sisters, my brothers and I would all fit the definition of orphans in matter of hours.

*It must be a bad dream,* I hoped. *It can't happen this way.*

Dad had passed away unexpectedly eight months ago. The scars were fresh in our hearts. The pain throbbed in our minds. The idea that Mom would give up everything on earth to be reunited with him was selfishly unbearable.

"I don't think the ice cream is good anymore," Mom said. "I wish I could have kept it in the freezer for you."

How beautiful. How sad. In her final hours, Mom continued to look after her perfectly healthy son.

In the end, I guess, the proudest possession a parent owns is an abysmal sense of sacrifice, complacency and gratitude. I did not want to cry, but tears began to drop.

"We had worst days than this," Mom assured. "Things will be all right."

I'd wanted to hug her, but only managed to reach for her hand—the hand that shaped and molded me into the person I am today. As we held hands, mom talked about the weather, family and, oddly enough, a pairs of scissors.

"The blade of a knife may be sharper than that of the scissors," she said. "But the scissors can cut fabric exactly the way you have envisioned."

In her own way, Mom ingrained in us lifelong, guiding principles through parables. Her ordinary words would later become our sources of profound wisdom. Mom paused for a second as she gazed outside the window.

"The scissors, with its two dull blades, cut beautifully," she continued, "while the knife and its single razor-sharp edge can't even make a straight line."

"I'm sorry, Mom. I'm not following you."

"The brightest stars are merely a reflection of the sun," Mom explained. "But the sun alone fails to let us see the majestic beauty of the nights."

As she spoke, golden light danced through the window blinds. It gave the room a warm glow. All sounds seemed muffled. Maybe it was a prelude that the angels were ready to guide Mom home.

"What I'm saying is, son, don't go out in the world alone," Mom concluded. "Lean on your brothers, sisters and your friends."

Those were Mom's last words.

Since that day, our family has never been the same. We don't seem to see each other as often as we used to. But I notice the bonds among us strengthen as each day goes by. When we laugh, the smiles are brighter. And when tears fall, we hug longer. What holds us together is a kind of endurance that comes from a sense of satisfaction knowing that Mom gave us her all.

Now it's our chance. It's our turn.

I was told that time heals everything. What I have discovered — since mom's death — is that the passage of time only deepens my hurts and widens the respect I have for her. It has been more than fifteen years since that unforgettably heartbreaking event happened. But it is not long enough for the cut to stop bleeding. Perhaps, it never will.

My feeling about this loss has been and ebb and flow of sadness and joy and back. There are times I blame Mom for my many sleepless nights. I miss her so much that the loneliness fools me into believing that Mom will be at the door any moment. All I need is another chance to tell her how much I love her. And all I desire is to be embraced in her loving arms, to be a kid once again.

Then there are times when the daily pressures seem overwhelming. I just close my eyes and think of Mom. The thought that she is in a better place now brings great elation to my heart. No more headaches. No more suffering. No more fear.

Then there are times I catch myself sitting by the door, waiting silently and patiently for her.

See, Mom? It's past midnight and I am still here listening for the doorbell. I guess you are tied up somewhere with Dad and won't be home soon. I'd better stop crying and go to bed.

Good night, Mom.

"I can shake off everything as I write; my sorrows disappear, my courage reborn."

ANONYMOUS

# love is

SHELENE ATANACIO

*mahal kita* in Tagalog, my native tongue
what holds us up when we are too weak to stand

like a fire-breathing dragon paving its way
an unstoppable force that fuels us to move mountains

*mahal kita*, my ancestors can show you
a lifelong lesson, experiences felt

the instrument that draws two into a slow dance
each breath strung together into a chorus

*mahal kita*, a warm body that wraps around you
a language that everyone can speak

"Dads don't need to be tall
and broad-shouldered and
clever. Love makes them so."

PAM BROWN

# Understanding a Father's Love

I LOVE YOU. In Western culture, these three words are used all the time, whether to a lover, family, friends, or even pets. Can one feel and express love without saying "I love you"?

Growing up in a strict traditional Chinese family, the word "love" was rarely used. My parents have never told us they love us, and I have never heard my parents say "I love you" to each other. They were not physically affectionate with each other publicly nor were they physically affectionate with us. Instead of thinking this odd, I always wondered why it was so simple for others to say "I love you." It seems to naturally roll off their tongues, like "Hi, how are you?" or "Please pass the beans."

But I had to admit there was something nice about a family being so outwardly affectionate with one another. I would watch with envy as my friends' parents showered them with hugs and kisses and asked them "How was school today?" When my parents picked me up, there were no affectionate greetings. Instead, they would bombard me with questions such as, "Did you behave in school today?", "Did you cause any trouble for the teacher?", "What did you learn today?", and "Did you do well on your tests?" They never seemed to really care about how I felt and were more concerned whether I somehow bought shame to the family. My friends were given weekly allowances for doing well on exams and doing chores. However, getting good grades was my job and helping out with chores was my responsibility as a member of the family. The only time I received money was during Chinese New Year. When I asked why my friends were able to have a TV in their room or allowed to watch TV during school days, the answer would simply be: "You get what you need, not what you want."

My father has a muscular build with broad shoulders and a stern look, so at first sight he can be quite intimidating. He is a man of few words and rarely expresses any emotions. When I was a child, he was a hands-off dad. He never attended any parent teacher conferences, participated in any of my school activities, or attended any of my school performances. He felt these things were frivolous and impractical and only took time away from my studies. This lack of affection and encouragement manifested into a lifelong struggle to constantly seek his approval. I also questioned whether he knew how much I loved him.

The kitchen was more than just a place where my family gathered to eat. It was where I spent most of my childhood and youth. I did my homework, studied for tests and prepared for my SATs. It was also where we spent the most time together as a family. It was usually over a meal in the kitchen where rules were set, problems solved and important issues discussed. Most importantly, it was there that I began to recognize what love meant for my father. Growing up, my mother used to tell me that to capture a man's heart you had to capture his stomach. I did not quite comprehend what she meant until I started to take interest in cooking. I also discovered that food is an expression of love for your family and friends. There is nothing more loving and nurturing than fueling one's soul with food. Through the process of cooking, I gradually found that saying "I love you" out loud is not the only way to show you love someone. I also began to understand my father's way of love.

My father would never say, "This food is delicious!" but cooking for him and watching his lips curve into a small, content smile as he ate gave me a much-needed sense of accomplishment. I learned which dishes he likes best: those that are hearty but uncomplicated, requiring few ingredients. And he does not care for fancy presentation or frivolity when it comes to his meals. In these ways, his favorite foods are much like his way of love. While he oftentimes sits through the entire dinner without uttering a single word, I slowly began to realize that he was savoring the time with the people he loved most, and he didn't want to spoil that feeling of gratification with idle chatter.

This lifelong journey led me to appreciate that his way of love was based on practicality. Love for him is a responsibility that cannot be fully expressed in three words. Instead he displays his love by making sure the family is well provided for, and that we are well equipped with the tools to navigate through the complicated society we live in. He instilled in us a sense of constant security, an anchor in even the roughest of waters. There is no need for too many words. I can always count on him to deliver and carry through anything that is asked of him.

I was finally able to see through my father's eyes that expressing your love for someone comes with great responsibility. Truth to be told, I have also never told my father I love him. Yet, I know my father does not need me to tell him I love him, but what he does expect from me is to be the best that I can be in the different roles I take on, whether it is fulfilling the duties as a daughter, employer, wife or future mother. For him, that is the best way to express my love for him.

It has taken me quite a long time to feel comfortable saying the words "I love you." Now that I am a mother, I tell my son I love him often. But I have inadvertently learned through my father that the words "I love you" are sacred. They should not be taken lightly or used haphazardly unless you are willing and able to take on the responsibilities that come with them.

"The finest thing of all about friendship is that it sends a ray of good hope into the future, and keeps our hearts from faltering or falling to the wayside."

MARCUS TULLIUS CICERO

# What I Did for Pho

Once upon a time there was a Vietnamese restaurant. And then there were two, and four, and eight, until one corner of downtown had hundreds, all clumped together and indistinguishable. Little Saigon was one of the first. It's the one I always went to, maybe once a week, usually with my wife Phyllis. One Sunday we went down for a late lunch and walked straight into the wrong restaurant. We didn't realize it until we had the menus in our hands. Identical menus, only these menus were spanking new.

"They didn't change owners?" Phyllis asked.

I looked at the menu cover. It said "Golden Saigon." I looked around and realized that all the furniture was ever so slightly different, the colors brighter on the wall. We walked outside and looked at the building.

"Look, there's Little Saigon," I said.

Golden Saigon was smack next to Little Saigon, the doors only three or four feet apart. If you weren't careful, you'd walk straight into Golden Saigon and never know it wasn't a part of Little Saigon. Even the sign was in the same yellow color, same style, same size.

"Clever," Phyllis said.

We went into Little Saigon and ordered lunch. Mr. Nguyen, the

31

owner, came out of the kitchen and greeted us warmly. We told him what had happened to us. Mr. Nguyen's blood pressure shot through the roof. He started choking out Vietnamese sounds.

"Can you believe the nerve? Can you believe the nerve?" he spat. "I work hard, work very, very hard to establish my restaurant. It's a good restaurant, I have a good clientele, we work seven days a week— we work sixteen hours a day, my family, for ten years and they have the nerve to steal it! Just steal it! It's highway robbery. How can this happen? Why do they let this happen in America?"

We shook our heads in sympathy.

"It seems silly to have the same restaurants all in the same neighborhood," Phyllis said. "It happens all the time. All the Chinese restaurants are right next door to each other. All the Korean and Mexican. There's a street with five burrito restaurants where I work."

"Crazy. Crazy. The world is crazy," Mr. Nguyen said. "I thought it'd be different here, but it's worse."

"I wish there was a Vietnamese restaurant where we live," I said. "I'd eat there all the time."

"Where do you live?" Mr. Nguyen asked.

"Uptown. Near the 60s. Why isn't there a single Vietnamese restaurant past the bridge?"

"We've all got to stick together," Mr. Nguyen said. "Safety in numbers. It's crazy. Now we can't make money. None of us can make money. There's only so many customers. It's crazy. We used to be full all day. Now we're lucky to have a full house during lunch. Our food's good, but we're not as cheap as the new noodle houses. Cheap ingredients, cheap food. I'm not even going to tell you where they get their fish. I wouldn't let my cat eat there. I never buy anything but the best. I have pride. They have customers. Why eat cheap food? I don't understand."

Mr. Nguyen was always modest. The food at Little Saigon was the best. It was Mr. Nguyen, his hawk-eyed fervor. He knew what every one of his customers was eating, how much, what they left behind. And if you left even the tiniest morsel, he was there at the table like a shot, asking what was wrong. His specialty was the noodle dishes. There were fifty different kinds of pho alone, rotating on a daily basis in accordance with what was fresh that morning.

"So here's a suggestion," I said. "Why don't you open up a restaurant uptown?"

"No," he said, waving his hand. "All the customers come here for Vietnamese food. They wouldn't go uptown."

"If you moved up, they would."

"Rent's higher. Wouldn't make money."

"But you could raise your prices. They expect to pay higher prices uptown. You'd be the only Vietnamese restaurant around. No competition."

Mr. Nguyen laughed. More customers came in and he went to greet them.

About a month later, I noticed one of the restaurants in my neighborhood had closed. There was a "for lease" sign on the window. It was a small intimate space, right across from where I lived. Done right, it'd be a perfect place for Mr. Nguyen. I just couldn't let it go. I called Mr. Nguyen and persuaded him to come up and look at the place with me. I pitched him the idea again, and since I'm a graphic designer, I told him I'd draw up the plans for the interior for free. The more I talked, the more persuasive I got. Finally, his eyes lit up as the idea took hold: An upscale Vietnamese restaurant.

"I have to talk it over with my wife," he said. But I knew he'd caught my bug. I knew I had him. The best Vietnamese restaurant in the city was moving across from me, and I couldn't be more excited.

Hammering out the details of the lease was a nuisance, but after Phyllis's brother, the big-time lawyer, got involved, things happened quickly. I had my pals move in and we practically gutted the place. Spanking new kitchen, the stainless steel shimmering like a mirage in the desert, funky fun furniture, warm wooden floors, huge panes of glass etched with shimmery gold paint, bamboo leaves and birds evoking glamorous orientalism. My friend Alice, the landscape artist, did that for free. She loved her pho, too. In fact, all my pals were doing things at cost—we felt part of something important. Like we were making some kind of declaration, although exactly what that was, none of us could really say.

The grand opening was a complete success. The Nguyens laid out an emperor's buffet and we partied until two in the morning. Phyllis and I'd sent out invitations to half the town. And of course there was the neighborhood, people who'd been curious for weeks, their eyes peeping in through the big panes of glass, pointing to the sign and asking when, when, when? Some were already fans of Vietnamese food, others had never even heard of it. Phyllis and I had sometimes stood for hours outside the door proselytizing. For those of the brave who ventured inside, Mr. Nguyen handed out tiny samples of spring rolls. Or cups of iced Vietnamese coffee. Tantalizing them for the grand opening.

The next day was business as usual. I couldn't admire the Nguyens enough. The entire family stayed up all night to clean up the place. By lunch time they were open and greeting guests. The restaurant was booked solid the entire first month. For dinner. Lunches were a hit-or-miss affair. Most of the businesses were a few blocks east and people were still slowly finding out about the place. And like I said, some people weren't quite sure what to make of it. I sat at the bar for lunch every day. The Nguyens wanted to give me everything for free, but I wouldn't hear of it.

Working from home, the hop over to the Nguyens' was too easy. Pho, a cup of Vietnamese coffee, snacks—I was constantly running across the street for something to eat. Once, I ate five bowls of pho in one day. It wasn't unusual for me to sit at the Nguyens' all day long, working on the laptop, nibbling on spring rolls. Finally, I had to make myself go less. Limit myself to once a day. I was really putting on the pounds. Phyllis could never understand my fanaticism.

"There's only so much pho a person can eat," she said.

"Speak for yourself."

About six weeks after the Nguyens' grand opening, my workload doubled in one of those freak cycles and I forgot about the restaurant. I was living off yogurts and pizzas-on-the-run between meetings. And then one night Phyllis asked me if I'd gone past the Nguyens' lately.

"Of course I've gone past it," I said. "I pass it every day."

"Yeah, but have you looked inside?"

"Looked inside?"

"Yes, big boy. Looked inside. They have no customers. The place is completely empty. All day long."

"What? That can't be."

"See for yourself."

I ran into my office. From there we had a perfectly clear view into the Nguyens'. Phyllis was right. I couldn't see one customer.

"Hmm. Let's go over for dinner," I said. "See what's going on."

Mr. Nguyen was sitting at one of the back tables reading a newspaper. The place was a ghost town. Mr. Nguyen greeted us warmly, a rueful smile on his face.

"It's been a while, Tom," he said.

"I've been so busy with work—this is the first time I've eaten out in weeks. Phyllis will tell you—I've been living off yogurts. I can't tell you how I'm looking forward to this."

"Sit here. At the best table, as usual."

"So how's everything?" I asked.

"Well, as you can see, business is slow. Very, very slow."

He got us a couple of beers and started pouring.

"But I don't understand. Things were so good."

"Yup. Yup. Sometimes that happens. When a restaurant is new, everyone comes. And then sometimes they forget about it. People always want something new. Novelty impact."

"Novelty syndrome," Phyllis said.

"Hopefully it'll pick up soon," I said.

"Yup. Hopefully."

I was truly distressed. Making up some excuse, I went back to the apartment and started calling everyone I could think of.

"It's an impromptu party — you have to come, now. Quick or you'll miss all the fun. We're having a huge banquet at the Nguyens'," I said. "The Nguyens'. Our Vietnamese restaurant. Yes, that one. Yeah, they do have great food. Have you gone back since the opening? Yeah, yeah, I know. Me, too. I've been living off yogurts. Listen, call everyone you know. See you there!"

As soon as I got back to the restaurant, Phyllis took her turn, calling up everyone she knew. By nine o'clock, the restaurant was filled with revelers.

But you can't have a party every night. Phyllis and I started having almost all our meals at the Nguyens'. We cajoled our friends, even strangers, into making reservations. I met my clients there, even if it was just for coffee or drinks. I knew a friend who was a friend of a restaurant critic. She wrote a favorable review. I got them listed in tourist guides. I did everything. But the damn restaurant was cursed.

I didn't get it. How can you have great food, good location, and empty tables? I couldn't get any work done. I'd just stare at the restaurant from my desk. It got to the point that Phyllis and I would avoid walking past the restaurant. We'd go around the back block. We were so ashamed; we couldn't even show our faces. After all, it was our fault. We'd persuaded Mr. Nguyen to close up a perfectly good restaurant to move all the way uptown for what? Our convenience? Only we'd really believed it'd work. Why hadn't it worked?

In only eight months the restaurant was closed. God, it's a cruel business. The site stayed vacant for several years. My heart skipped a little every time I saw the "for lease" sign. We didn't know what happened to the Nguyens. We were too ashamed to try to find out. And then three years later, Phyllis and I ran into Mr. Nguyen. He was working as a waiter at a Vietnamese restaurant near Chinatown, one his brother-in-law owned.

"It's so good to see you," we both said, genuinely happy. "We'd wondered where you'd gone. How's your wife?"

"Fine, fine. She's working at a dim sum restaurant nearby. Maybe by the end of the year, we'll have enough money to open another restaurant. We'll see, we'll see."

"Oh, Mr. Nguyen," Phyllis said, breaking down.

"We're awfully sorry about what happened," I said. "We should never have talked you into moving uptown. I can't tell you how bad we feel about the whole thing. If we could only make it up to you— but I imagine you don't want anything to do with us, considering—"

"Not a problem, not a problem," Mr. Nguyen said, curtly. He sort of waved his hand, as if the past was a pesky fly.

# Kimchee and Schnitzel

Four years ago, my sister invited me to a dinner at a lovely Italian restaurant in Los Angeles. She said we'd be dining with some friends visiting from Austria. I gladly accepted saying, "I love Australians!"

I walked into the restaurant, and there in the middle of two extremely sun-burnt and gorgeous men was my sister. That's when I fell in love with Thomas, the *Austrian* on her right. (I figured it out when he sounded more like Arnold than Crocodile Dundee.)

From the very first night we met, we both knew we had met each other's match and had fallen deeply in love. However, after a year of pure bliss, his working visa had run out and he asked me to move with him to Germany. I agonized over the same question the Clash had contemplated in the 80's: "Should I stay or should I go?"

I had traveled all over the world, taking long treks to Asia, Australia, Europe, Central America, and the Caribbean, but never, ever did I live anywhere except Los Angeles. A two week vacation to some exotic isle or country is quite different from packing all your belongings into four suitcases, leaving all your friends, family, car, lifestyle, customs, and language to move to a very, very strange place, called GERMANY!

All I really knew about Germany was that they made great cars, led in soccer finals, ate sauerkraut and produced Heidi Klum. But I was moving for LOVE and it was all or nothing. Just like in the movies, I picked everything up to be with my gorgeous, future Austrian husband. We were in love and the world was our oyster.

How wrong I was! There were to be no oysters; in fact, in Germany there was hardly any seafood at all. Germans are not into venturing out too far into the culinary world, and their idea of a good time was a jug of beer and a greasy schnitzel. They are also creatures of habits and they are very happy eating this several times a week. (Greasy schnitzel is number 86 on my "100 Reasons Why I Hate Germany" blog. I think I am on reason number 246… )

For Koreans, food is the binder that keeps us all together. It brings us to the dinner table for actual conversation or arguments, it gathers families for holidays or celebrations. My mother, being the head of a large household, was the Chef. Perhaps growing up near China helped her master the art of Korean, Chinese, and Japanese cooking. Her culinary prowess turned every meal into a feast. Thanksgivings were a potpourri of different cultures: turkey, kimchee, chapchae and fried shrimp tempura—my favorite. Korean food is not just for pleasure and nourishment. It defines me.

So when I learned that there was not a single Korean restaurant within 100 kilometers of our cute little apartment in our new home of Baden-Württemberg, I began a new obsession of finding Korean or any types of Asian foods. Thomas and I racked up thousands of kilometers driving all over Germany trying to find somewhere to get our fill of the ever-addictive Korean homemade spicy beef Yukejang soup.

However, this was not sustainable. We couldn't continue to drive across the country every time one of us got a craving for something besides a pretzel. I had to learn how to make my own meals. Now, I wasn't totally new to the kitchen. Back home, I had ventured into the land of Martha Stewart and Emeril Lagasse, but I had not yet stepped foot into the elusive territory of Korean food.

Living in Germany didn't help either. There were days I could not find a green onion, or spring onion as they call it there. And many markets didn't even carry cilantro or jalapeño. I drove or took the subway or U-bahn to every place I heard that might sell a Korean red pepper paste. Everything is outrageously expensive. I paid 300 Euro for a rice cooker in Dusseldorf. And the task of buying Korean ingredients is almost impossible. I had to order most of them online. The trouble is that the two languages used to describe them were in German or Korean, which, by the way, I am not fluent in. But little by little, I started to conquer the cooking of my homeland.

So, although there are 246 reasons I hate Germany, there is one thing I am grateful for. Living in this land forced me to discover my roots—mainly my turnip roots. I finally learned how to cook. I'm making sauces from scratch with an Asian pear, cooking a mean soon tofu broth and hot *dukboki*, Korean rice cakes smothered in red pepper paste.

I won't say I'm as good as my mother—that would take sixty years— but I learned that with a good computer, a good cookbook, a good appetite and an open mind, it's possible to conquer the challenges of fine Korean cooking—even in Germany.

"Behind almost every great
man there stands either a good
parent or a good teacher."

GILBERT HIGHET

# A Drive Home

San Diego, California. June 2011.

Heading home from work long day long week busy year so far.
The drive fifteen minutes best time for catch-up with myself it's
needed with children. All three one girl two boys she's five they're
two I know...

Turn right Deerskin Drive the suburbs country town San Diego.
Straight ahead dry hills mustard color golden yellow hay and wheat
wild artichokes.
Need rain.

Children impatient they're waiting.

Their faces my girl a princess pink dresses pink gowns pink shoes
pink bows pink gems on crown.

My twins a scientist the other don't know a swordsman maybe perhaps.

The scientist he's quiet quite reserved "to himself" loves puzzles building blocks pushes buttons the DVD the vacuum cell phones the iPad iPod i-Buttons.

The swordsman a riot quite active loves sticks the longer the better he protects the princess.

Drive up this hill carefully slow neighbors wave kids pause time out car's coming dog walkers sprinklers tick mustard grass brown grass dead grass.

NPR on. Reporter talking host interrupts Libyan freedom live broadcast casualties report. Son dead father crying father bereaved crying louder dead son father's arms.

Reporter speaks cracked voice "he's grieving" "great grief" background sounds machine guns AK rifles bombs blown people yelling and screaming father crying in background.

Radio static.

"You're breaking." "Please repeat."

More static guns blast background sound too windy broadcast disrupts radio static.

Too noisy. It's frustrating. Somewhat annoying. That's war. I know. Radio off. News off. Tragedies off. Noise off. The wars. On, off.

Windows down long week gaze ahead mind wanders suffering world.

I remember Danang Vietnam family escaped fishing boat typhoon season dodged bullets machine guns background noise AK rifles Tat, Tat! Tat, Tat!

Grenades blown Boom, Boom! I remember always do always will a detriment bitter-sweet triumphant.

The beginning only five sagas continue long story beautiful life beautiful struggle.

Libya Vietnam Vietnam Libya I regress compare contrast too noisy it's frustrating somewhat annoying that's war I assume I know same story.

Inhale deeply shake head frightening memories divert thoughts tell myself "forget yesterday" "live today" I can't I've tried damn PTSD life's happening many triggers takes effort takes love.

I reframe. Coping mechanism.

Those faces beautiful faces my faces bright smiles buttermilk teeth button noses slanted eyes all me I know…

Turn left Aladdin Way slopey hill 200 yards they're waiting I'm waiting for me.

New day old thoughts always conflicting I'm scared anxiety sets daughter's five my age back when Saigon fell her beginning only five.

I regress bullets grazed I ran by myself fishing boat there waiting with sister mother's arms and ran and ran dear life only five I ran dear life.

The beginning. New day. Old thoughts.

These days princess runs for fun from swordsman different life different game I progress.

Almost there sweet home children await those faces beautiful faces innocent souls not knowing Daddy's journey my war kept secret still there still inside internal war on, off. Turbulent memory painful journey keep walking.

I see outside house from distance three characters cartoon characters three kids not mine. Na ah, not mine…Are they?

Just yesterday thirty years I'm them.

Six eyes look up see me my car.

They jump up, down "Daddy, Daddy!" three kids they're jumping fingers pointing at me.

Not mine nah ah not mine I'm them.

Pulling up the curb my house.

Scientist pouts then cries Princess dances on grass no care Swordsman points his sword a stick a branch at me.

"Daddy, Daddy! Come out!" Princess demands.

"Who's 'Daddy'?" Not me.

I sit and look at them…at me.

Those faces my eyes my nose my brows my smile my skin.

Three Lacs. One girl. Two boys.

"Daddy's home!" Princess screams.

"Ya, ya!" Swordsman points his sword and shouts.

Scientist frowns head down rubs eyes big pout.

"What's wrong? Little scientist?" I wonder I see I feel it's me in him.

"Don't cry my son Daddy's here." Yes, 'Daddy' your father.

I know kids cry get sad get confused on days I understand.

My father he didn't.

My siblings and I during childhood loved running loved pretending loved playing loved noise. Pa said no running no pretending no playing no noise. Just study only study no interaction.

Damn PTSD. Damn depression. Damn paranoia.

Often times I fake my happiness growing up. No cries it pisses Pa off he said be strong stay strong move on no time for men immigrant men to cry.

Pa's right. Great words of encouragement. Different time. Different circumstances. Different life.

My Pa my boss my supervisor my general no signs of affection no intimacy no bond no hugs no kisses no words of sentiments he's allergic to closeness to tenderness to "feelings" of love. A kid his son longed for the reassurance the encouragement the words the acts of sentiment.

Grew up longing searching to fill this void this emptiness. This love.

It takes few words a hug an embrace; the luxury cultural luxury social luxury generational luxury; I know.

The feeling the void the emptiness Scientist needs my touch his father my embrace his father my affection his father my words my promise my presence my empathy I am his father.

I inhale.

I understand.

I know.

Swordsman runs to car with sword a stick a branch in hand.

Princess follows.

Scientist stays rubs eyes.

I say, "Princess, Swordsman; what happened to Scientist? He's sad never leave your brother your sister in time of need."

My father told me the same.

Step out of car.

"Hi, Princess." "Hi, Swordsman."

"Daddy, Daddy please dance with me," Princess asks.

"Ya. Ya!" Swordsman pokes his sword at me.

"Hey, Scientist." "What's wrong?"

I approach Scientist he's frowning or pouting it's sadness a child.

I take his hand sit down on grass with him.

Scientist knows, he knows, he asks—though non-verbal—I know, I give…

I'm him.

"Come here Princess, Swordsman sit down with us."

Princess obliges Swordsman doesn't.

"Ya. Ya!" with stick his sword in hand.

My arm around Scientist "You're sad? Don't be; be happy I'm sorry to be at work."

Princess listens then imitates, "Don't cry it's okay Daddy's here."

I turn Scientist's head to me; he's sad his frown puppy eyes.

"You're sad? Don't be, be happy." I say.

"Yeah, Scientist, be happy." Princess reiterates.

"See, there; your sister the princess loves you."

I tilt my head toward Scientist's and hug him tight.
Princess imitates.

The swordsman sees us the three of us we're hugging. He joins.

"See, there; your twin your brother loves you," I whisper.

The four of us. We're hugging.

To them I say with conviction.

"I love you."

"Lucky parents who have fine children usually have lucky children who have fine parents."

JAMES A. BREWER

# Love Demonstrated

Well, I just said whatever came to mind," I said, chuckling. I could hear my mom's laugh through the phone, and I paused, reflecting for a brief second before I realized how positive she'd responded to my story. Then again, I knew that she and my dad had probably heard all sorts of tales in the last twenty-eight years in the United States, when they had to manage however they could as immigrants to a new country.

I had been telling my mother about my first weeks at Harvard. She'd asked about new friends and the students who attended graduate school at the university we only imagined I'd ever get to attend. I'd told her that most of the students I'd met were quick to point out that their parents were either prominent lawyers or medical doctors in their respective hometown cities. Without flinching, I replied to their inquiries, "My mom is a housewife, and my dad is a self-employed electrician, carpenter, and handyman." I guess I didn't hold back because at that moment of truth, I knew where I came from, and how far I had come. I was reminded that I was a part of the same university as sons and daughters of fancy-occupation parents. Responding openly to my classmates was just another lesson in the process of learning to become more me.

Jokingly, my mom advised me to say that she was a professor of "Home University" and my dad a lawyer, or "The Law." I laughed, but a part of me knew she just wanted me to feel comfortable on Crimson grounds, so that I could study and not think about anything that would shake my confidence or self-esteem at a prestigious Ivy League university.

That brief conversation stayed with me throughout my time at Harvard. She didn't have to say what she did, but she did it anyway. I understood her efforts to support me, even if I was 3,000 miles away.

It wasn't until I participated in the Higher Education forum on "Privilege and Power" that I was able to mentally re-package what I had already known for a long time. I knew my roots and my birthplace in Los Angeles. I knew my upbringing. I knew my family, and I knew the opportunities and privileges that I was given. The privilege game only directed participants to "step forward one step if you did not have to worry about money throughout your childhood" or "step forward one step if you had a car in high school." As my classmates stepped forward based on their privileges, the disparity between my classmates was visually apparent. Who cares if I was only one of two standing in the back of the room because I did not have the same privileges as my classmates? The privilege game unveiled more explicitly that I was privileged in many other ways than the cars, allowance money or other tangible things that my classmates received as children and teens. I was given privileges to think freely, learn continuously, and live graciously.

Each time in my life when I came across difficult situations, my mom and dad would enforce the sense of pride and confidence that surpassed the need to retreat in tears or shame. This time, my eyes watered. I swallowed my tears, tasting salt in my throat. I didn't want my classmates to see. I wasn't ashamed, but I'd just realized more of my purpose and I was eager to explore it in private.

When I got back to my fourth-floor dorm room in Child Hall, I retreated in a tranquil reflection of what had happened. The experience was translated in a few minutes of blank stares to my white, painted brick walls, and I was even more understanding of my parents' hardships.

I honestly think that it took me ten years to really figure out what love means in an Asian American family. I feel like I was cheated by the television programs that showed parents hugging their children, and rattling off the line never heard in a Chinese family, "I love you."

My family immigrated to the United States in 1977, and my fourth brother and I were born as U.S. citizens soon after. My parents and three older brothers brought with them a few suitcases and a whole set of dreams to fuel their unknown journey in a new world. My mother carried a picture of Kwan-Yin, Goddess of Mercy, which was hung on the wall and blessed our home throughout my childhood years. She knew that it was going to be difficult, but I don't think she was ready for everything that she and my father had to endure with my four older brothers. Nonetheless, my parents pushed through and put all five of us through school.

When I was in elementary school, I learned that if your parents made you cupcakes, you were loved. I thought love was having a packed sandwich, like the ones I saw other kids had in their lunch boxes, and the hugs and kisses they got on their foreheads before the bell. I learned that if Santa came to bring you presents on Christmas, you were loved. I didn't know that love came unconditionally without price tags and without gaudy, showcased gestures at that age. But now, it's different. I know what it is.

Love, to me, is the strength and wisdom my parents gave me. Love is the shared messages of support and care. It's the purposeful joke to provide comfort. It is sometimes wrapped in something a second-generation Chinese American girl couldn't decipher at first glance. In essence, I can guarantee that the package is much more worthy than a sweet treat or mass-produced toy. I was told that as a Chinese American, you have to work twice the efforts of another person. "You have to work harder so you can get to the same level of prestige and impact," they said. They believed in me. They expected my success because they worked by hope, not by money.

I faithfully believe I am loved in so many ways. I'm sure they would say so, too. Besides, who is to argue with a professor and a lawyer?

51

"Okay, we are different it's true.
And I don't like to do all the things that you do.
But here's one thing to think through,
You're a lot like me and I'm a lot like you!"

ROBERT ALAN

# On Happiness and Hapaness

These days being of mixed heritage is not uncommon. I feel fortunate to have grown up in as diverse a place as Southern California, but being mixed still contributed a great deal to my struggle with culture and self-identity. I have never had a solitary ethnic background to identify with. Those infernal forms with the little checkboxes that want you to identify your race are always very confusing to me. Am I "Caucasian," "Asian," "South East-Asian," "Filipino," or "Other"? As I entered adolescence, not only was I trying to find out who I was; I didn't know what I was.

My mother came to the United States from the Philippines when she was twenty-seven years old. She came to work as a nurse and met my father, a California raised German-Austrian American who was briefly her patient. A couple of years later they were married and had three kids, the youngest of which was me.

My Filipino grandparents, my Lola and Lolo, came to live with and take care of my siblings and me until I was ten. I spent my days playing with my cousins or otherwise wedged between my Lola and Lolo on the couch as they watched the Filipino news, waiting eagerly for my mom to finish cooking *sinigang*. Filipino aunts and cousins constantly surrounded me as a child; whereas on the other hand, my father's only living relative was his father who we visited from time to time. My father had completely succeeded us to my mother's culture since he had little to share of his own. Up until my pre-teens, I identified with the Filipino culture just as much as many of my Filipino American friends did.

Our family gatherings were small, but when I think of reunions I more fondly recall the parties that my mom's friends had; the mountain of sandals by the front door, unrestrained female laughter echoing somewhere in the background, waves of delicious smells of noodles and barbeque floating from the kitchen, the way that the hosts' house felt open and welcoming and alive. My siblings and my father and I were never treated as if we were different. When we were together, we were all family, blood and heritage aside.

Towards the end of elementary school, I admit that media influenced my ideals. I longed for the platinum blond hair my father had, perhaps a straighter nose like him, and bigger and greener eyes. Then as I entered middle school and my group of friends switched to predominantly Asian, I wished I was shorter, thinner, and lighter skinned. Towards the end of those years, I bounced back and forth between the two groups feeling sprawled across a cultural no-man's land. At times, I felt certain aspects of my life fell between the gaps, and I ended up feeling jaded and outcast. It is a time in development when we all feel a little alone and confused, but this was made all the more salient to me by my quest for cultural identity.

When I was thirteen I took a trip to the Philippines for Christmas vacation with my entire family. I had been there as a baby, but this was the first time I could actually remember, and it was a wonderful experience. I was reunited with my Lola and Lolo after three long years, and aside from some commentary on how tall I was, everyone welcomed us with open arms. I remember feeling so strongly connected to everything and everyone, even relatives and family friends I had never met, as if all along we had been joined by strings that were at long last being drawn closer together. During my stay, I experienced some of the most meager conditions. Yet, even when living in this less-than-ideal environment, these relatives and their friends seem to exhibit a culture of optimism, resilience and faith. They kept their chins up, a dance in their steps and song in their hearts. I was surrounded by family, delicious food, and laughter-filled conversation in both Tagalog and English. I witnessed a culture of optimism, resilience and faith. Family is a top priority and both friends and strangers are always greeted with kindness. It's a part of my culture I've come to adore and hope to be forever tied to.

As I grew older I realized our culture does not define us, but rather culture is the foundation, the bow that shoots us off and initially guides us. Where we land is up to the bow and the unpredictable arc we must fly through. Everyone struggles to find their place in the world. We hold it in our hearts for so long that we need concr words and labels to define ourselves, when all we really need is ou. all encompassing name and sense of self.

In the end, I feel like a pieced together conglomeration of American, Asian, and Filipino. I have finally somewhat mastered the skill of bringing out the strengths of each in different situations, and I've developed a pride rather than an ambivalence towards my background. I'm grateful for my heritage! It has made me open to and knowledgeable about many other cultures, and I would not have it any other way.

> "When a friend asks
> there is no tomorrow."
>
> GEORGE HERBERT

# unjaded

## TRACI KATO-KIRIYAMA

approach me with an unfastened mind
ready to be ravished by the entertainment
of all absurd ideas and lashings to religion

come with me to lay against the base of willows
and rediscover the truth underneath our shadows
as we exchange questions with fiery abandon

we will declare an attack on trademarked labels
and two-for-one seminars aimed at the weary who
wish for nothing more than to be told an answer

we will promise to feed a path of simple complexity,
agree we are surrounded my common originality,
and unfathomably understand nothing is as it seems

love me with an unjaded heart and a softened soul
ready to be taken by none other than yourself
and in that trail you blaze, i will follow

"The most unfortunate thing that happens to a person who fears failure is that he limits himself by becoming afraid to try anything new."

LEO BUSCAGLIA

# Against the Grain

My mother always told me that I was allowed to choose any career I wanted—as long as it met with a mile long list of conditions. Basically, the career had to be stable, produce a healthy income, and specifically not be a career in writing. "IT JUST HOBBY!" my mother would always say when I told her I wanted to be a writer.

But, ever since I could write with crayons, I knew exactly what I wanted to do in life: write. To me it was an exciting passion. To my parents, it was a challenge to their traditional, Thai parental authority— especially to my mother.

Even after I'd won local writing contests, published personal essays and opinion pieces, and wrote for several national and international publications, my mother insisted that my writing career was "JUST HOBBY!"

To make matters more confusing, my mother always preached that as long as I excelled and believed in my abilities to do anything, I would succeed regardless. Now, I wasn't sure if my mother was supporting me, trying to baffle me, or if she was challenging me.

I took it as a challenge. I was determined to prove to my mother that my writing career was substantial, it was real, and it was not just something I do for fun in my spare time.

For years, I had held a job that kept me neatly and quietly tucked away in my personal safe haven of an office. The job itself was fine, but it was undoubtedly holding me back from reaching my full writing potential. It was time to pack up and accept my mother's challenge.

Within a week of applying for writing positions, I was invited to an interview at Panasonic Avionics Corporation, one of the major divisions of Panasonic. Two days later, I received an offer that presented an interesting dilemma. I had to quickly make the choice to leave or stay at my old job.

The catch was that it was the job offer was only for a temporary position, with no guarantee that I was going to be with the company permanently. This work fulfilled not one of the criteria on my mom's list: it wasn't stable, it wasn't terribly lucrative, and it was a job in writing. I accepted it.

Within a few weeks, I not only excelled above and beyond my supervisor's expectations, but I was hired as a permanent member of the Panasonic family.

To my mother: Khun Mae, thank you for the challenge.

# Meat Loaf & Mashed Potato

As I was growing up, I recall watching a decent amount of television. I also remember noticing that most shows — from *Full House* to *Family Ties* — would end in a touching, heart-felt moment between parents and children, siblings or friends. Each party would express their love for the other with a direct "I love you," followed by the inevitable group hug. In my head, I would initially think "C'mon! Really?! I mean, *who* does that?!" But somewhere deep in my heart, I would often wonder, "Why don't *we* do that?"

Both of my parents immigrated to the United States from Japan during the 1960s. Since they were only in junior high when they arrived, they had a decent amount of time to adapt to their new surroundings. By the time my sister and I were born, Mom and Dad were pretty Americanized: they spoke English in the house, Dad loved big, American cars, and Mom would make meat loaf and mashed potatoes for dinner. The one seemingly American custom they did not acquire, however, was this direct and physical expression of affection that I would so often see on TV. As young children, our parents hugged and kissed my sister and me when they dropped us off at kindergarten or tucked us into bed. But as we moved into early childhood, such gestures gradually came to an end.

It became apparent to me at an early age that public or outward displays of affection were frowned upon in Japanese culture. Verbal affirmations like "I love you" were unheard of. Grandparents would never squeeze my cheeks or shower me with kisses. A slight bow or wave would suffice as a greeting among relatives. I learned to accept this general aloofness as the norm in my family, so I never expected anything more. But in middle school, when I would see my friends receive good-bye hugs from mom or overhear "I love you, too!" as they were getting off the phone with dad, I couldn't help but wonder how it would feel to be a part of such a close-knit family.

Now that my husband and I are preparing to start our own family, we've had a number of discussions regarding parenting, schooling and disciplining. While some issues have yet to be decided, others, we plan to figure out as we go. There is one area, however, where I have already made the executive decision, a choice which came about earlier this year when I was casually meeting with a friend. She and I were sitting in her kitchen chatting when her two year- old daughter pranced into the room. Without missing a beat, my friend wrapped her arms around her little girl, planted a kiss on her head and said, "Oh, I love you!" Watching the child's reaction simply made my heart melt. Her eyes instantly lit up. Then a wide, toothy grin spread across her face as she chimed back, "I love you!" While this may have seemed typical to some, I was utterly delighted and touched by all the warmth and fuzziness in the room, so foreign to my more traditional, Japanese upbringing. In that moment, I made the conscious decision that saying "I love you" and an abundance of hugs and kisses would be the norm in my future family, and not limited to the toddler years.

If my children ever happen to come across a rerun of those television shows I watched as a child, the thoughts going through their minds should be something as "Wow! They're just like us!" I am extremely grateful for the many aspects of Japanese culture my parents and grandparents have been able to share with me, and I hope to teach my children everything I have learned about the language, traditional foods and customs. The longstanding aversion to the display of affection, however, will be a part of my culture I will not be passing on.

# There's No Place Like Home

I suppose you could say I've always had a nomadic spirit, one that's always wanted to experience other cultures, meet new people, "see the world." I took my first journey as a two year-old when I wandered off several blocks from home. A kind neighbor eventually found me crying for my mom, and several door knocks later, returned me safely to my parents. I was too young to have any recollection of this, but apparently my wandering nature was set before I even knew it.

My first adult adventure took me to Eastern Europe. I visited a village in Bosnia on a spiritual pilgrimage, which transformed my life profoundly, allowing me to settle from a deeper place within. Even still, the travel bug remained. I had a list of places I wanted to see in my lifetime. The following year, I found myself jet-setting throughout much of Europe to places like England, France, Germany, and Switzerland. During the following years, I ventured through more of Europe; yet, although I was thoroughly captivated by the picture-perfect landscapes, I did not feel complete. Everywhere I went, I was still somehow unfulfilled. I couldn't express what I was looking for exactly; all I knew was that I hadn't found it.

I tried to explain this lack of fulfillment to a friend, who shared this sentiment with me: the more he travelled—while he learned much about other cultures and lifestyles—he learned even more about himself. In looking back on my travels, I realized that I was looking for a place to call home. Not necessarily a physical home, but rather a place where I could be fully and completely myself, and was able to live out my purpose, whatever that might be. I hadn't found that place in the green calm of Switzerland or on the clear, refreshing shores of the Mediterranean.

What of home, then? I started thinking about traveling to my homeland, Vietnam. I was born in the U.S. following my parents' immigration from Vietnam after the war. Even though I had never set foot in our native country before, there was always a part of me that felt a yearning to return, and hopefully understand my roots on a deeper level. Maybe I would find home there. Yes, Vietnam would be my next adventure. I would spend some time volunteering with various communities and then hop on a tour throughout the country.

There is a term for Vietnamese who grow up in the U.S. or move to the U.S. and come back to visit—*viet kieu*—and the locals can spot them right away. Simply by the tone of their skin, the way they walk, even the way that they smell. My language skills only confirmed this for them, since I could speak Vietnamese conversationally, but clearly with an American accent. On paper I was Vietnamese, sure, but I completely felt like a foreigner in my own country.

Still, I was in the motherland. I saw the home where my dad grew up, the church where my parents were married, and the streets they used to walk. I learned why traditional dresses, as I had been told, from my mom's region, *Hue*, were a deep purple—it was the school uniform color for girls who lived there. I also learned why my parents would keep so many items around the house that seemed unnecessary, such as stored grocery bags or saved jars. In Vietnam, many people never had enough. I began to see how their life in Vietnam led them to carry the values of saving, practicality, and so much more, into their new life in the U.S. In these small moments, I began to understand the larger picture of my parents, their background, our culture.

What fascinated me the most, though, were the people and subsequent conversations with them. More than any of the magnificent or richly historical sites I visited, it was the story of their day-to-day life that gave me a richer picture of where I came from. I would learn of the man who made not more than $20 US Dollars per month. With half of the money going to gas and one-third to his son's tuition, there was barely anything left over to cover food and other necessities. I would meet the old woman who would provide tours on her paddle boat through a distance of several miles. And there was the family that would wake up hours before dawn to meet the farmers to pick their produce, in hopes to sell a few bushels that day in the hectic market. It seemed so many Vietnamese could barely get by, yet there were also business owners who would drop hundreds of dollars on a bottle of liquor. The stark differences struck deeply as I began to see more clearly that we had similar desires: to provide for ourselves and loved ones, for a sense of security, for happiness. Wherever life was taking each of us, I came to see that our deepest yearnings were essentially the same.

My trip to Vietnam made me ask myself on a much deeper level, *who am I*? Where am I meant to settle and live out my purpose in life? But the answer that I received was different than what I had expected.

When you're in a completely foreign place, you come to know who you really are and what you're made of. In Vietnam, I realized on a deeper level that everything I'd been looking for has been and always will be within. What was I searching for? Peace, joy, fulfillment, purpose. Not only would I not find this in any place out in the world, I would not find it in any other person or thing either. I came to understand that what I was searching for was within me, and by taking time and creating space to listen more attentively, I would be able to discover more of what was there all along.

Funny how I had to travel halfway across the world to "find myself," as they say. I came as a tourist, but left with a deep sense of one on a journey. The main journey was not about the distance traveled on an airplane but to a deeper place inside myself—the only place I can truly call home.

"If you really want to make a friend, go to someone's house and eat with him... the people who give you their food give you their heart."

CESAR CHAVEZ

# Super Sandwich

My red, plastic My Little Pony lunchbox looked like everyone else's at my grade school, but once opened, it told a different story. My mom packed fried rice and pork sung in Tupperware she'd bought at a local swap meet. The Ziploc was full of sliced up pig ears and cow tongue. And to wash it all down, she included asparagus drink and chrysanthemum tea.

As the only Asian heritage American kid in the entire school, I experienced a range of emotions about my lunch, from shame and alienation to gleeful joy at how grossed out people got when I told them I liked the way the cartilage of the pig ears crunched in my mouth.

I must have mentioned something to her about my lunch being so different from everyone else's, because one day it started to change. I observed with passive intrigue at the way my packed lunch evolved, morphed, and mutated as my mother expressed her interpretation of "American" between two slices of white Wonder bread.

Her logic was really very simple. She saw the flimsy PB&Js and baloney & mayo sandwiches and thought, "That's not enough." Especially not for her voracious daughter who was always asking for seconds and thirds or more of everything.

One day at lunch, a friend of mine peeked into my beloved Pony lunchbox. "What is that?" she asked.

I pulled my sandwich out and unwrapped it from the Saran. My tiny fingers could barely hold the three pieces of bread that capriciously held together the pork sung, fried egg, rice, pickled lettuce, and whatever else that had been leftover from last night's dinner, all carefully glued to the insides of the sandwich with peanut butter and jelly and glops of mayonnaise. I tilted my head as I looked at the monstrosity I held in my small hands, trying to categorize it, label it in a way that would be comprehensible to my peers, to myself.

"It's a super sandwich."

"Oh."

It made total sense.

"Is it good?" another ventured to ask.

I held the abomination to my mouth, opening so wide my jaw was in danger of unhinging, my fingers working hard to flatten the slices of bread and the entire bento packed in between them. The bite was big, the crunch of random ingredients loud, the peanut butter and jelly sealing the deal and my mouth as well.

Nodding, I let out a "mmhph" of approval.

After swallowing the first bite, I was feeling generous.

"You want some?"

Faces screwed up and turned away.

I shrugged my shoulders. "More for me."

Every day the sandwich was different. Every day I wondered what delightful surprises awaited me between those slices of white Wonder bread.

Over a decade later, I finished college and moved out for the first time on my own.

Tired of eating out at the same old places after our wushu class together, I lamented to my boyfriend, "I feel like a super sandwich."

"A what?"

I explained the scrumptious glory that could added to a plain PB&J. He looked at me with doubt in his eyes. I resolved to make him one right away. As I used peanut butter and jelly to paste the fried egg, lettuce, and tomato to the insides of butter-and-sugar fried bread slices, my own special super sandwich recipe, I could tell I was testing the boundaries of our relationship. I could see the trepidation in his eyes, the look that asked if I was the Akane to his Ranma.

When I handed him his first super sandwich, he dutifully picked it up and took a bite out of it with a substantial amount of apprehension. I could almost see the flavors melt into his mouth as his eyes widened with surprise.

"It's good!"

Though my red, plastic My Little Pony lunchbox is long gone, Mom's creation and teaching continue. "Take the best of both cultures and make it your own," she often said in her mother tongue. So, whenever I crave for comfort and love, I turn to my super sandwich.

"Eat up," I smiled widely.

"If you can see your path laid out in front of you step by step, you know it's not your path. Your own path you make with every step you take. That's why it's your path."

JOSEPH CAMPBELL

# Bridge Through the Strange Forest

As an avid student of Shinnyo Buddhism, my personal philosophy can be summed up in the quote on the previous page.

By not even being aware of it, I have always encouraged myself to be more involved in my respective community and be mindful to assist others without expectations of specific rewards or results.

A wise woman, Shinso Ito, once said, "Making a contribution does not only mean donating one's time or money: it also means to live actively amongst others. It is to be engaged with the surrounding community, to become aware that there are things we can do."

As my passion for social action through art and entertainment progressed, I realized that the journey to find my purpose in life would soon be discovered.

My fervor for visual arts stemmed from my first visit to the Museum of Contemporary Arts in Los Angeles when I was thirteen. I'll always remember that the exhibit that stood out to me the most was the *Strange Forest* concept designed by world-renowned Japanese artist Takashi Murakami. I was overwhelmed attempting to observe how these magnificent pieces were conceptualized. It was as if Murakami had the ability to take each of his patrons into a hallucinogenic, twisted world filled with amazing color detail and diversity.

Murakami's vision combined fine quality, extraordinary detail, and unique simplicity in order to portray a contemporary Japan through the eyes of a child. The amazing thing that really jumped out at me was how The *Strange Forest* could illustrate very clearly Japan's problematic history and cultural development.

If such an abstract exhibit could make perfect sense to me as a young teenager, I was more inclined to believe that art could transcend cultural boundaries and effectively communicate a powerful message if executed the right way. This experience assured me that my passion for cultural art would start to blossom, and I took it upon myself to break down and analyze each figure from a theoretical perspective.

My understanding at the time was that subconsciously, artists such as Murakami were attempting to convey a message within their work in order to communicate to those outside of their own culture. However, the challenge was to effectively convey this message to transcend the social boundaries, and the stories behind the art should somehow communicate beyond its cultural matrix and speak directly to our common humanity. My understanding and affection for visual arts grew to understand this notion as my knowledge for art theory matured.

In the 1990's when social media (let alone the Internet) was in its infancy phase, the idea of transcending social boundaries was virtually impossible to execute unless an artist was considered prominent amongst his culture or society. If such a platform existed that would allow artists from all over the world to view the history and values of other people through their cultural and artistic background, surely we could use it to promote global understanding.

Over the last few decades, the world has become more developed and interconnected through means that we would have never imagined. Now, artists have learned to utilize these online resources to construct virtual bridges and platforms to share their work and as a result, the social media movement has effectively streamlined human interchange.

As time moved forward and my personal project designed to build awareness for the respective Asian American community continued to develop, I realized how effectively the Internet has changed the way the world has communicated with one another. It was remarkable to witness how the new generation of artists constructed a kinship within their niche. Musicians from different parts of the world would somehow get together and collaborate in order to produce a well-constructed composition, and filmmakers from different backgrounds would collaborate to create a beautifully filmed motion picture. This is how my animated film, "Hibakusha", came to fruition. Nowadays, artists do not have to go through terrestrial radio or television broadcasts to get discovered. Social and online platforms have provided the necessary tools for them to expand their networks and multiply the numbers of their following.

Now how does all of this connect to my practice in Buddhism? One word. Love.

Love brings out the best in people, and it is a reflection of one's self to be linked through this same belief. Love is what motivates people to become better and improve themselves to reach ultimate bliss and eternal happiness. But it is ultimately love that makes people drop their own egos and work together in a search for fulfillment through any means. I have always believed that art was essential in communicating a universal reality, simply because I consider it to be a language that all human beings share in common.

The Channel APA network that my friend and I have built together in the last few years allows for the new Asian American generation of artists to create peace and harmony through their art between people of all races, countries of origin, and religious beliefs. My experience working with these creative people in the last six years has really inspired me to change the world by building bridges for these artists to connect with each other and participate in a consistently growing movement.

As I am continuing to walk my spiritual path, I have always embraced the three altruistic practices of generosity, service to others, and sharing the Dharma. By helping to create an Asian American art and entertainment network for the people who truly embrace the sincere meaning of love, I have come to connect with young and talented artists for the greater purpose of changing the world.

# Taboo

MIN K. KANG

1. In Korea red ink is reserved for the dead.
   I wrote my mother's name in red ink
   after I was sent to my room
   for behaving rotten. "When you sleepover
   at an American's house, you come back
   as a different child."

2. Upon discovering frames of family photos
   next to white candles on a dresser,
   I was asked, "Why have you set up
   a shrine for relatives who haven't died yet?"
   I shrugged, insisting my friend should
   let go of her old country's ways.

   Only after she left, I moved the frames,
   scattered them throughout my home,
   hoping to undo the bad fortune.

3. On the floor we sat around the dining table,
   cross-legged. It was set with my favorites,
   steamed eggs, blanched spinach, fried fish.
   Table was set for three, but my sister and I
   started eating. Grandpa arrived minutes later,
   scolded us for not waiting for him to eat.

   It hurt that he cursed my dad for failing
   to teach us to wait for him to eat,
   but I kept hogging the fried fish on the table,
   picked at the crispy flesh
   until there were only bones left.

---

4. Number 4 is unlucky in my language,
   sounds too much like "death."
   Grandparents owned a motel—
   it had no fourth floor, only fifth.
   I knew the truth—I stayed away
   from that floor anyway.

   When I had to replace bars of soap
   and fresh towels on that floor,
   I threw the toiletries into the sink,
   ran for the stairs
   as quickly as possible.


5. Every 25th of June we were told to draw
   pictures of a reunited Korea—
   of children holding hands across
   our rabbit-shaped peninsula.
   We studied the Korean flag in the room
   to recreate onto our white paper.
   What no one told us was how
   we'd grow to forget the Buk-han children
   or how the refugees can never shed
   their terse, cold accents
   nor their cheekbones, which are as high
   as Baekdu Mountain,
   set against
   their sunken cheeks.

"Cooking is like love. It should be entered into with abandon or not at all."

HARRIET VAN HORNE

# What I Won't Do Pho Love

For my mother, Le Anna, and sisters, Trinh and Sonja.

I'm your typical half-Vietnamese, South Carolina-born guy that was raised with a mixture of strict Southern Baptist ways and harsh Asian roots. My father was a Southern American Caucasian and my mother is a Vietnamese. They moved to the States a few years before I was born. As far as I knew, I was a Southern white boy. But I sensed early on that my brown skin did not quite fit in with the white and black world that surrounded me. My freckly complexion stood out when Ma took us to the Vietnamese events around our region. The white kids looked at me funny; the Asian kids looked at me funny. As a very young child in the early 80s, it was confusing to not be accepted by either side of my heritage.

Still, I was happy.

It's already difficult being a kid, looking for acceptance, trying to find where you belong in the world, and having the desire to love and be loved. At five years old, I started school and it became apparent that I did not look like anyone else. My classmates didn't quite know what to make of me but they left me alone. Kindergarten was okay.

First grade was different. Recesses began and challenges surfaced. Being of Asian descent, I soon learned that just about every kid at the school assumed I knew karate and therefore wanted to fight me. As soon as we hit the playground, a circle would form around me and four, five, six, sometimes even more, kids would take turns swinging at me to see if I could fend them off. Although I never took a karate class in my life, I was able to dodge and deflect most of their punches. It was a tough way to experience childhood. Eventually the fights and challenges sputtered out. Perhaps, the novelty wore off or because they got to know me and we became friends.

At the end of first grade, my father died from cancer and left behind my mom, my two older sisters, and me. The pain was tremendous. At the age of six, I became the "Man of the House." Despite the endless struggles, Ma was able to keep a roof over our heads and put food on the table. My father was a meat and potatoes guy and my mom learned to cook those kinds of meals well. But there's one dish — a Vietnamese dish — my mother made that not only fed our family and gave us the nutrients we needed; it also comforted us and held us together. When I hovered over a large bowl, the steam engulfing my face as I slurped up noodles and broth, nothing mattered in the world. At that moment I felt no pain; I belonged there.

As I continued to grow up in the South, many ridiculed me for who I was not while others accepted for who I am. The constant in my life was the unconditional love of my family. Many times I kept my struggles to myself because I knew my mother and sisters had plenty to deal with as well. But all it took was a simple hug and a bowl of pho to make me feel that I am who I am supposed to be and that those who matter accept me wholeheartedly.

When I was eighteen, I left South Carolina to attend a college in Tennessee. After graduation, I made my way to Southern California. On my way, I made a pit stop in Dallas, where my good friend Carlyn lived. While I waited for her to get off work, I sat in front of a Kentucky Fried Chicken, realizing this was the furthest I had ever been away from home. I was scared and I thought, "What am I doing?" So, I called my Ma and told her I was turning around and driving back home. She said, "It's not like you're moving from Communist China. If you don't like it, you can come back." What Mom was referring to was the decision that she'd made to leave Vietnam at twenty-three so that her children — unlike their mother — would have a better future. She knew then she would never see her family again. So, to honor her sacrifices, I pressed on, seeing more of this beautiful country in three days than I had seen in my whole life.

When I arrived in Los Angeles, I was overwhelmed by the sheer magnitude of the racial diversity. People of all races live side-by-side with one another while maintaining their own heritages and cultures. I discovered China town, Korean town, Japanese town, and many other towns that made me feel like I was in another country.

The first few months were difficult. I was the lone country boy — both frightened and excited — in a big city. Then 9/11 happened. Alone and without friends, I was lost. I was told to not come into work so I had nothing to do, nowhere to go. I didn't want to sit around in my tiny apartment while the nation was being shattered by the events of the day. So I drove around for hours. The city was a ghost town. But I noticed that there were pho restaurants everywhere. There was "Pho 2000," "Pho 24," "Pho LA" and "Pho Café."

I had hit the jackpot.

From that day on, whenever I feel homesick or alone, I find the nearest pho restaurant. I hover over a bowl of rice noodles submerged in a steamy broth, redolent of star anise, freshly torn basil and sliced beef. The familiar flavors comfort my soul. As the steam engulfs my face, I am once again taken to a place where all is right with the world. And the spiciness of the soup that causes beads of sweat to form on the bridge of my nose brings me back to where I once again feel whole.

I had only planned on staying in Los Angeles for a year before returning to South Carolina as an "adult." But I had established a career in television and was doing what I loved, so I stayed. And as the years went on, I met other people like me. There was Giang who also had a white father and Vietnamese mother. The same day I met Giang, I met Thuy and Kalena who taught me what a "hapa" was. ("Hapa" is a term used to describe a person of mixed Asian heritage.) And I had my buddy Tam who was always eager to throw down a good Vietnamese meal with me. Over time, I met more bi-racial and multi-racial people. In my late 20s, I finally realized that some of them had similar stories to me and that I wasn't alone in being a child of mixed cultures. And it's a different time now as more and more multi-racial people are becoming prevalent and more visible.

I just passed the ten-year mark here in Los Angeles. I've hit my stride in my life and found my place in the world. My career has given me the ability to travel and to live in the three biggest cities in the country: New York, Los Angeles and Houston. I still miss South Carolina because my friends and family are there. Fortunately, I am able to visit them a few times a year. I bet you know what I ask Ma to cook for me. But when home remains thousands of miles away, I turn to a West Coast bowl of pho for comfort. I've learned to make a pretty mean batch myself, too.

In fact, think I'll go have a bowl now.

# Ode to the Chinese Male

Yesterday while in Beijing's expat district Sanlitun, I proposed a theory to my hairdresser. The reason why there were disproportionately so few Chinese men with foreign women couples is that the same distinguishing features about Asian people that make Asian women so attractive to foreign men: they're smaller, softer, and sweeter—are the same qualities that unfortunately render Asian men unattractive to foreign women.

Many of the qualities of Chinese culture, when placed side by side with Western culture, are *feminine* in nature: the modesty, the submissiveness, the importance placed on harmony, family and community. Western culture, and by extension Westerners, are comparatively more independent, assertive, exuberant and into violent, team sports like American football. American football will always symbolize the West for me. The game blazes and roars in a way that makes it the last thing I can ever imagine any Chinese people ever taking up.

While my Chinese hairdresser agreed, he also proposed, with a smile, that it's also a case of Chinese men not being into foreign women.

While I am 100% ethnically Chinese, apparently my Australian upbringing has stamped a sort of "masculinity" onto me. Previously

I designed a little thought experiment in which I placed my photo among eight Mainland women and asked readers to see if they could pick me. As I was dressed in clothes I had bought in China, and had carefully chosen a mix of Chinese women from different classes, I had assumed people would have trouble. But to my surprise, commenters overwhelmingly claimed that they'd instantly picked me. One person had said my build was more "athletic" (at 165 cm I would be considered on the big side by Asian standards—although I have always been "average" in Australia), while another said that I seem less gendered (that is, less "girly").

Despite growing up in Australia and so surrounded by burly, outdoorsy types, I've never been into super masculine men. As a teenager my heartthrob was the slender Leonardo DiCaprio, as seen in Baz Luhrmann's *Romeo and Juliet*. So perhaps it's unsurprising that unlike most foreign women who come to China — including overseas born Chinese women — I discovered that I was quite into Chinese Mainland guys. I love how they text you every hour ("I just ate breakfast," "it's hot today," "I just ate lunch," "what are you doing to eat for dinner?"), I love how soft their skin is; but most of all, I just think some of them are really pretty.

A good friend of mine — a true, blue Aussie sheila if you've ever seen one — has a thing for Asian guys. It was a novelty to me, to be in China and be able to share "hey check *him* out" comments with a white girl. We once travelled together from Beijing to Dalian and mutually confessed a crush on the same ticket inspector. All the characters who starred in her love life were Asian—as is her current boyfriend. And this one, a hunky Chinese lifeguard from the local pool, has been her most serious relationship to date. She has what you call "Yellow Fever."

But typically the term references white men who have a taste for Asian women, because it rarely so happens the other way around. A video of the same name, made by some Chinese American filmmakers, takes some funny jabs at the subject as noted in their own country. In the video, the Chinese American protagonist finds his sister has been too easily seduced by his white flatmate. But by the end of the video the tables have turned, when the same sister suddenly goes all lovesick at the sight of his black friend.

Africans are an increasingly common sight here in Beijing, and if the contrast between a white person and a Chinese person, I'd argue that it is even more so with Africans. The timbre of an African voice resonates deeply. And his form is generally more muscular, while the physique of the Chinese man next to him either seems to disappear into the folds of his shirt, or else cradle a cheerfully round beer belly. All in all, Africans are highly noticeable in a wash of Chinese faces.

And Chinese men with African girlfriends or wives are a novelty that many internet commenters here sarcastically attack. A purvey of these comments shows the lack of political correctness and outright racism that exists in China in regards to black people. I'll never forget one Chinese class we were reading a textbook in which the Chinese author described a character as a "beautiful black woman," which made my teacher laugh. She said, "I guess the writer is just being polite." When I asked her why, she said, "Uh, well, I guess we Chinese people can't tell if a black person is beautiful or not."

As crudely as she said it, I can't help but think that for all the foreign women that come to China and turn their noses up at the locals, a healthy mixture of open-mindedness and natural acclimatization would help change their minds. My Polish friend Matty used to think all Chinese people look the same. Once when we were on the Beijing subway he jokingly pushed our Chinese Peruvian friend Anthony back into the crowd of Chinese people, and then said, "Anthony, where are you? I can't see you!" The bastard. But after two years in China, Matty says this isn't the case for him anymore.

One's eye can be accustomed to the Chinese look, to the point that I feel unsettled in the first day or two of each holiday I spend in Australia. The men there seem too tall, so broad-shouldered, so pale, and so very hairy. Moving to China and digging the local guys belongs to a wider process of cultural immersion. I speak Chinese, eat Chinese food, watch Chinese television. Isn't it natural I also begin to like Chinese guys as well? It annoys me when foreign women openly say Chinese guys simply aren't attractive. Rather than qualify that it is *they* who don't find Chinese guys attractive, seeing as attraction is a matter that is purely subjective.

The last Chinese boyfriend I had once cheekily slapped me on the bum and told me I was bigger than him, which I was. Being with him was how I imagined it felt like to be in a male, gay couple. It wasn't simply a cultural subversion in some ways it felt like a *gender subversion* as well.

Perhaps it's fair to say on a traditional scale of masculinity, Chinese men come up comparatively short. But I don't need a guy to hunt boar, plant potatoes, build my house with his bare hands, or fight wars. I need a guy who will be my partner. Be a good father to our kids. Hold my hand, and hug me when I feel sad that I'm living so far away from my family and friends. And for these things there are many attractive Chinese guys who definitely qualify.

# Think Before You Text

Texting is a great communication tool. But like any tool, texting has limitations. It can only do so much. Sometimes, it can do more harm than good, especially when we try to text something that plays on our emotions. Even when people are face-to-face, there's always a risk of a misunderstanding and conflict. Tone of voice, facial expression, body language, eye contact, mood are all important clues that help us know how the other person feels, and they cannot be translated in a text message.

Think about it. Has a text message you sent or received ever been misunderstood? Did either of you get hurt? Have you heard of relationships ending because someone got the wrong impression?

I have.

Let's look at a text from "Him" to "Her." He likes her, so he texts to ask her out:
Him: *"Want to hang out?"*
Her: *"Sorry, doing something."*
Him: *"OK."* Or he doesn't reply.

Now, let's look at some ways he might think and feel about her reply:
- *"I'll try again later."* Feels okay.
- *"Maybe she's teasing me."* Feels happy.
- *"She didn't say no. Maybe she likes me too."* Feels encouraged.
- *"What's she really doing?"* Feels anxious.
- *"Why didn't she tell me what she's doing?"* Feels confused; suspicious.
- *"She doesn't want to be with me."* Feels rejected, sad, a little angry.
- *"Forget it. She'll probably has a boyfriend already."* Feels hopeless.

Take some time, and think about the different ways she could think and feel about his text too.

As a therapist, I know that conflict in face-to-face relationships — intimate partners, friends, colleagues, classmates or family — can erupt like a volcano. During couple's counseling sessions, a subtle change in tone of voice, a glance away, or a misunderstood remark can cause suspicion or an accusation. Logic and reasoning aren't effective when emotions flood the room, and the heart. And like lava from a volcano, the flow of hurtful emotions is hard to stop. One thing is for certain—I never tell people to work out their differences by texting. Instead, I tell them to stop.

Reducing emotional pain requires that both people recognize each other's emotions. When they learn to 'hear' and accept each other's feelings, they feel respected. They feel safe. Conflict no longer includes pain or rage. Let's compare the results of hearing words and reading text when a fight seems to have no end.

Imagine that you're in a close relationship. You've been fighting about one thing for several days. Neither of you see a way out. Think about how you would feel if, instead of a text, your partner calls you and says:
- *"Right now, we might not know how we'll solve this and move on. We're both hurt and angry, and I hate to see you suffering. I wanted to tell you that I'm right here, with you, and I'll do all I can."*
- Even though the fight isn't resolved, would you have hope for the relationship?

In the early stages of an intimate relationship neither person knows the other's 'love vocabulary' so the risk for misunderstanding is greater. Realizing the playfulness or concern or joy or pain or anticipation intended by the message may not happen.

This can be even more of an issue when people from different cultures try to relate by texting. Cultural norms and ways of interpreting and expressing feelings are often different. So get to know someone from another culture personally before you send him or her texts.

Women frequently say, "He doesn't hear me." Men complain they don't understand why things worsen when they try to 'fix' the problem.

Take the time to think about these questions:
- How can someone 'hear' you in a text?
- How can your partner know you care without hearing your voice or looking into your eyes?
- How can texting really fix a relationship problem?

Some helpful hints:
- Don't assume someone should, or will, know what you mean by your text. People seldom think or feel the same way.
- Don't expect someone to correctly interpret what you're feeling. No one can read your mind, and you can't read theirs.
- Do not rely on texting when working on a group project.
- If you think it's important, it is. Call or meet instead.
- Don't try to text your emotions. The other person won't know you're mood.
- Don't text each other during a fight. Texting usually makes it worse. Loving feelings are seldom, if ever, successfully conveyed by texting.
- Text messages are not confidential and can be accessed—forever. If you don't want your message online now or in the future, change it or don't send it.

Retuning to our first example, let's look at another possibility:

Him: *"Want to hang out?"*

Her: *"Sorry, doing something."*

Him: *"OK. I'll call you later."*

# My Heart

NEELAM CHANDRA

I have a heart
Of pure butter
Which melts at every
Thought of compassion and care
Love dwells in every
Nook and corner of my heart…

My love
For you
Is hidden deep inside
In a valley of adoration
Come dear sweetheart
In this gorge of passion
And let the purity of the butter
Take us into a world
Where
Affection
Tenderness
And fondness
Shall submerge us
Into ultimate bliss…

"My father gave me the greatest gift anyone could give another person, he believed in me."

JIM VALVANO

# My Father's Gift

The sharp siren pierces through the traffic noise on the crowded street. I pull over to the curb just as the fire truck rumbles past. My heart flutters and feelings of dread and anticipation slowly spread. I turn off the engine and take a couple of deep breaths which instantly calm me and send me to a place of comfort where the sound of siren resides in another place and time...

...It was nearing the end of a war that had torn our country apart. The fighting between both sides had escalated dramatically. The city where we lived was no longer a peaceful place far away from the battles that raged in countryside around us. We were more often awakened by the sound of a siren piercing through the night—the pulsating, shrieking racket that got us out of beds and into the underground shelter behind the house. When I hopped down from my bunk bed, I bumped into my sister in the lower bunk and instantly got a shove from her. Before I had a chance to raise my voice in protest and push back, my mother shushed us and my father herded us and our younger siblings out of the bedroom, across the family room, through the screen door to the garden and ducked quickly into the underground shelter. My widowed aunt and her son as well my older brother and sister were already there.

This bomb shelter, a spacious make-believe kitchen or classroom for my sisters and me during our play, was now very tight quarters for our ten-member family. Though it was well past bedtime, I was alert and aware of the tension-filled silence enveloping us, punctuated by the explosions that were preceded at times by flares that lit up the dark sky. All of us sat on straw mats with our backs against the hard concrete, huddling and shivering in the cold damp air that seeped from the clay floor beneath our feet. I heard the soft whimpers from my baby brother as he buried his face in my mother's chest. A quiet sob escaped from my aunt's lips—her husband was killed in a fierce battle last year and her older son was fighting in another one somewhere. I clutched my older sister's arm tightly, the earlier indignation forgotten. As the sound of another explosion retreated, my father's voice suddenly filled the space around us. At first I did not register what he was saying but the warm and resolute sound of his voice was enough to settle my anxiety. Similarly, I felt my sister's body relaxed beside me. "*We are together. We are here together as a family. We are fortunate to have a shelter. This shelter will keep us safe. No matter what might come, we are together as a family. There is nothing to fear. We are alive and safe. We are very fortunate to be here, together...*" On and on, my father's voice filled us with a sense of peace and comfort in-between the awful deafening sounds that seemed to come closer by the minutes. It was as if we were enveloped in a collective security blanket. We felt safe, loved, and like we belonged together as a family.

Many years later, after I immigrated to the U.S., people sometimes ask what it was like living and growing up in a war torn country, amidst constant fighting and bombing. They don't believe when I tell them I had a safe, sound and happy childhood. Like kids in other parts of the world, I went to school. I had homework and studied for tests. I had friends and parties. We had beautiful parks and beaches. But I also experienced coming to school after a night spent in the shelter to learn that a classmate or more had perished when a stray mortar fell on their house. I found it especially hard seeing classmates coming to school with a white band wrapped around their beautiful shiny black hair, signaling the loss of a loved one. There was definitely a lot of anxiety and uncertainty living amidst political upheaval and raging war. But my father had the wisdom to create islands of comfort and love for us whenever he could.

I remember the times when we had a picnic on a mountain top or took a trip to the beach. Each time, he urged us to remember, to take in the sight, the sound, and the feelings of the moment. *"Look at the beautiful mountains around us. See how high we are and how blue the sky looks from here? And the air here is so fresh! Take a deep breath. Go on, breathe it in. Isn't it wonderful? Oh, and what a great lunch your mother has packed for us. How fortunate we are, aren't we? I want you to remember it—this moment, this place.... We are so blessed."* Later on, whenever we were in danger or caught in a precarious situation, my father would vividly describe those outings to comfort us. Each night that we were awakened by the shrilling siren and stumbled half asleep into the underground shelter, we were reminded again how beautiful and precious life was and how fortunate we were to be alive and together.

We clung on to these cherished images and tender feelings that my father instilled in us to survive the years when we were separated and scattered all across the United States; we came as refugees at the end of the war and our family was split into small units to be sponsored out of camps. As for me, those precious moments of beauty, clarity, and peace that my father had gifted us cultivated a sense of mindfulness and gratefulness. Throughout my life, I have been able to invoke and relive it to overcome moments of despair and desolation. The ability to draw forth from deep within us the reservoir of goodness, love, and comfort is what gives us resiliency to bounce back from life's trials and tribulations. This gift that I received from my father is what I tried to pass on to my own children—the conscious knowledge and mindful appreciation of life's precious and fleeting moments of beauty and love. When captured and treasured, they make a great life's companion.

"Sometimes the poorest man leaves
his children the richest inheritance."

RUTH E. RENKEL

# Men Don't Talk About Their Feelings

*"Tinh yeu cua mot nguoi cha rat bao la nhu nui thai son."*

There is a saying in the Vietnamese culture that expresses an unconditional, limitless love of a father to his children, its vastness reaching toward the sky's band of clouds, unbounded and forever towering—like that of the peaks atop tallest mountains in Vietnam, *Thai Son.*

This phrase was no more than words to me, just another ancient Vietnamese "ca dao." After all, my father worked the majority of my childhood to make ends meet, so I wasn't encouraged to learn the Vietnamese language or more about its culture.

I spent much of my toddler years looking out of our apartment's window, counting down the minutes to see my father home again. He was always happy to be home, happy to see that I'd done my homework, or made him dinner, usually consisting of peanut butter, jelly, and soy-sauce on rice with cereal to top it. I still remember the few times Dad came home with a new toy for me. He watched me rejoice with it, but in silence.

Things were even quieter in my family after the death of my mother. After a heated argument with Dad, my brother was sent to

New Zealand. I didn't understand why Dad acted as if nothing had happened. Wasn't he hurt that Mom had died? Wasn't he upset that Andy had gone?

It wasn't until my babysitter told me, "Vietnamese men don't talk about their feelings; it's not right. That's what a woman does" that I began to see why my brother and father behaved in certain ways.

One Sunday, Dad and I were lying in bed, talking about life. He was preoccupied with the air conditioning, marveling at how a turn of a knob would instantly provide cool relief on a hot day. I bravely enlightened him with my afternoon of wondrous epiphany—of how I'd flushed Snoopy the goldfish down the toilet.

"Oh my goodness! Why?" His eyebrows arched.

"Because he was lonely, and I know he was sad. I learned in school that you shouldn't put trash on the streets because it drains to the ocean, like the toilet does. And in the ocean, there are more fish, so Snoopy can make friends," I answered.

My father boomed with laughter. I remember not being entirely sure what was so funny, but it was refreshing to see him expressing his emotions.

When I was eight, a woman came over to our apartment, bearing a giant box of Christmas-colored M&M candies, with bright mistletoe print splashed on the box's tin-can exterior. I accepted the candies with joy. She and my father laughed, and sat down on the couch. They spent hours this way, a few nights a week, talking and laughing in our apartment living room. *Strange*, I thought. *Who was this woman? And why did they always laugh when they were together?*

Four months later, my father told me we were going on a trip to Fresno.

"We're going to hang out with my friend and her kids. You'll like them," he said.

"But I don't want to go."

The words had escaped my mouth quicker than my mind could process, and I had no idea why I'd said it. I felt my face immediately grow hotter. I wasn't familiar with this feeling, and it didn't feel nice. My father breathed a heavy sigh. "You'll go, and you'll have fun, okay?"

I obliged.

"Why are we going? And why are we going with your friend?"

"Don't ask too many questions. We're going because…"

"Because what?"

"Daddy is going to marry her and you'll be the flower girl."

"But what about Mommy?"

"Kim," my father said in a hushed tone, "you can't speak like that anymore, okay?"

It seemed only yesterday that my father had carried me onto the hospital bed where my mother lay to kiss her chapped, chemotherapy-stricken lips one last time. Memories of her tossing me on her knees at our first home in Los Angeles replayed vividly in my head. I heard her soft voice, "Kim, you know I love you, right?"

Unexplained tears had rolled down my cheeks as I'd replied, "Yes."

Snapping back into reality, I answered softly as the car rolled on, "Okay, Dad."

Time went by, and my father and stepmother's wedding had passed. My new stepsiblings were of overwhelming presence to me. In particular, I clashed with my oldest stepsister, Katie, who was two years older than me. She didn't understand me, and I didn't understand her—and we bickered about even little things, frustratingly, until just about forever. I spent a lot of my afternoons crying, angry, playing by myself in the yard, cursing the fact that I was left out, or always told to stop whining, to "be the bigger person." *Why do I have to be the bigger person, when I am the youngest child in the house?* My eight year-old logic let it escape me and I resented being in my situation, not understanding why I felt so glum most of my days. School was my diversion to problems at home, and I did particularly well, even going on to be in state-wide math competitions and winning the spelling bee.

Some days, there would be so much tension with my stepsister; I would seek comfort from friends at school. At least with friends, I felt less judged; less like a black sheep, less pressure to just get it right on my first try. As my friendships at school strengthened, things at home seemed to worsen—the distance grew between my stepfamily and me. I fell into a bad pattern of hanging out all the time instead of coming home after the last bell had rung.

By the seventh grade, Katie and I had given up on talking to one another. Instead of sharing a room with my sisters, I moved to the back wing of the house. In the beginning, I didn't mind; it was a little freedom for me; a breather from blatantly being third wheel. But as time went on, the separation began to take toll. On most nights, I would get the call for dinner and arrive to see through the window that my family was already halfway through their meal. I would retreat cowardly to my room, sometimes forgoing dinner for my salty tears. I tried to push all of these feelings away, knowing what my stepsisters would say about my crying: *You're a drama queen; you're so sensitive, geez.*

I decided, with a knot in my heart, that I wouldn't be sensitive anymore. Well, not in front of my family, anyways. I felt I'd become a burden in particular to my father, who made such strenuous effort to smooth everything out at home in his own way—of trying to provide for me what he could. Pained and saddened, I turned to friends, and a boyfriend, an ultimately tumultuous relationship for a girl my age. Nonetheless, it cushioned and distracted me from the reality of my woes at home. Whatever spite and hardship came from friends and my boyfriend, however, it could never hurt me as deeply as the hurt I felt at home. I would deal, because I had no other choice.

*"Men don't talk about their feelings; it's not right. That's what a woman does."* These words echoed in my head again during this time that I'd made my choice to anchor my feelings to the bottom of my soul where no one could reach them.

*Well,* I thought, *I'd better man up.*

Soon after I made this vow, my tenth grade history teacher showed a film on the Vietnam War. To my fascination, I understood some of the things the speakers on the documentary said. It felt nice to learn about my homeland, and to feel a sense of belonging to my culture. Sprinting all the way home from school, with Ho Chi Minh's reign and the many astonishing escape stories fresh in my mind, I couldn't wait a second longer to learn about my parents' trip to America. I ripped through their drawers, where I knew they kept important documents. Surely, something *had* to be in these drawers that would tell the story of how we came to America. My heart raced to uncover all of the captivating details.

In drawer number one, I found many interesting things — my parents' wedding albums, our social security cards, our health insurance policies, my mother's wedding ring — but no exciting documents that gave way to our migration. Discouraged, I rummaged without much faith in drawer two. I came upon something. It wasn't documents indicating our boat trip, or plane ride, or source of arrival to America. It wasn't my father's war helmet, or a detailed account of the great trip to a new country. It was my handprint, in brown paint, with feathers glued onto the fingertip outlines. It was the turkey that I'd made in kindergarten, for Thanksgiving.

I touched the corner of a picture I drew of two stick figures: a stick with wiggly arms and hair in pigtails, and a man next to me, with a tie and glasses, almost triple my size. His shoes were black, with shoelaces longer than his arms. Across the top, messy crayon letters spelled out, "I LOVE MY DAD BECAUSE HE IS MY HERO. HE IS ALWAYS NICE, EVEN IF I MESS UP MY HOMEWORK."

As I uncovered layers and layers of drawings and photos, of little things I'd constructed with sticks and cotton, I began to sob uncontrollably. I wanted to be that little girl again, the one whose hero was her father, whose family was her world. I knew I had to be the change I wanted.

My initial attempts to apologize to my sister were shot down. But my efforts were fortified with time, age, experience and mostly—*love*. As I learned more about life, I developed an understanding about ideals and realities. For the first time, I saw the love everyone has for me. And then I dropped the walls I'd erected around my heart, allowing their love to come in.

And perhaps because of his belief that men don't express their feelings, my dad demonstrates love in a quiet, humble manner. In his own way, he has taught me about forgiveness and about growing above petty arguments. He does this instinctively, with love so readily available at any time, immeasurable, so limitless, so infinite in amount and size that it cannot be spoken at the risk of deafening by magnitude. It can only be compared to one thing—the boundless and forever towering peaks of the tallest mountains of Thai Son.

> "Nature does not hurry, yet
> everything is accomplished."
>
> LAO TZU

# The Fall Line

SANDY TSENG

The ocean is a skirt
of ambiguity

no one can recall
the hours over the water

in the plane poised
over the sea.

Why must we
move across time zones

the way we move
across powder—

the weightless body
pulling

in and out
of the mountainside

seeking the point
of balance / stability.

We are up to our knees
in the bowls

where moguls start
to form.

The momentum
commits us

even as the ground hardens
beneath our feet.

"Being deeply loved by someone gives you strength, while loving someone deeply gives you courage."

LAO TZU

# The Long Way Home

My parents often said, "Every lesson has a blessing." This phrase was merely a cluster of letters put together into words until one afternoon after a long day of classes. I decided to go to the help desk for a little Physics tutoring. I wasn't sure who the tutor would be as I headed towards the end of the hall down the Physics Department. I noticed that the door was closed as I got closer. Sure enough, as I turned the knob, the door was locked. I thought I might have misread the time and room location until a tall young gentleman came along. He was wearing jeans and a sweatshirt with his backpack on. His name was Bill and he was also a student studying at the University of Delaware. In fact, he was the president of the Physics Honor Society. He was a great tutor. I came in for help for the first two days of class and didn't feel the need to ask for assistance in problem solving for the rest of the semester.

I remember walking out of Physics class when my dad called me to inform me that my grandfather had been airlifted from Nevada to California. My heart dropped when I heard the news. Just knowing he would have to bear weekly dialysis through tubes and machines broke my heart. It was as if a dark cloud had formed above my head. Uncertain of what the outcome might be, I prayed and hoped for the best.

The summer my grandfather was hospitalized, my parents and I traveled from our home on the East Coast to the West Coast to be with him. Finally, my parents closed their business in Delaware and moved the family to Southern California. At that time, I lived in an apartment with three of my best friends and did not necessarily want to move across the country, but my family and I are very close. As Filipinos, our culture is well-known for having tight-knit families. And so I packed up and left with them.

I sat down on the chair across my grandfather's bed in the ICU of the University of Southern California's medical center every day that summer. His bed was surrounded by all the machines necessary to keep him alive, his heart rate to every pump of oxygen was monitored at all times. A white cotton shirt hung from his bony shoulder and shower-rod thin arms; warm blankets covered his swollen ankles and feet. He was in his fifth month of recovery from a lung infection after having undergone a lung transplant. "I love you, Papa," I often reminded him.

He softly whispered, "I love you, Patricia." His eyes, though open, were dim and distracted.

Holding his weak hand in mine brought tears to my eyes. I couldn't bring my head up because I didn't want my little brother to worry. I had to keep my composure to be strong for the family.

After five long months, my grandfather was eventually discharged from ICU. Although he may never be the same, his smile was as warm as ever. We moved my grandfather to a home in Ventura, California. His room had to be on the main floor because it had become too difficult for him to move his body like he use to or go up and down stairs. With his oxygen tank always nearby, his eyes sparkled as he looked up to see the view of the harbor from his window. He often sat outside in the evening to watch the sunset reflecting on the water as boats went by. As summer came to an end, so did his health. His strong spirit eventually became overpowered by his mortal body. He passed away peacefully in a deep sleep.

That September, on our way to the funeral home, I replayed all the childhood memories I shared with my grandfather. My grandfather was never afraid to show us how much he loved us through his warm affection. He was a man of many words, constantly reminding his grandchildren the importance of time and life goals. "It is never too early or too late to chase after your dreams," he said. I will never forget his words of encouragement and hope to pass it along to others. My grandfather was handsome, intuitive, creative, and someone I will always look up to. His smile was always sweet and genuine. As we got closer to the church where my grandfather's body lay, my vision of the world became hazed fighting to hold back my tears. I took a deep breath before walking in through the double doors.

I was startled by the loud and obnoxious ring of my cell phone. As I pulled my phone out of my purse to turn off the ringer, I was surprised to see the name Bill on the screen. Bill, the tutor who walked me through homework problems and Physics fundamentals from University of Delaware. Quickly, I answered the phone, and steadying my voice the best I could, I told him I would call him back. Although it took me a few days to return his call, I couldn't stop thinking about him.

Bill and I arranged to meet for dinner the following weekend. He explained that he had taken a job for a well known defense contractor in Los Angeles and was now sharing a townhouse with three friends in nearby Hermosa Beach. He took me to a restaurant on the pier that had a view of the sunset on the beach. I could now watch the sunset from Hermosa Beach that my grandfather so often watched from our home in Ventura. As I told him the story as to why I was now in California, the glare of the sunset on his bright blue eyes reflected hope into mine. We shared stories with each other and found a variety of things we had in common. He had a great sense of humor and was ambitious, intelligent, and most importantly, a gentleman. The connection we had was undeniable.

After several dates, he invited me to Movember, an annual fundraising event for men's health. This event involved the growing of moustaches during the month of November to show support for prostate cancer. I knew that saying yes not only meant I would be surrounded by men with creepy moustaches; it also meant that I was consenting to our first weekend together.

It had been some time since I'd last seen Bill. While driving through the freeways of L.A. from Ventura to Hollywood that night, I questioned all the events that had led to this. I could only hope I was making the right decision. Bill had asked me to meet him at the hotel lobby and said he would be wearing a white suit. As I crossed the street and came closer to the hotel entrance in my four-inch black stilettos and little black dress, there he was. As handsome as ever, moustache included. As I fixed my dress, he put his arms around me and looked into my eyes. "Trish," he said.

I had always wondered what love felt like. My grandfather had taught me that love was about respect and admiration; but then again, I respected and admired the Pope, and I certainly had no interest in him as a future mate. When I was a little girl, I asked my mother, "How will you know it's love?"

She replied, "You will just know." And I did. I was in love with Bill.

To this day, I am able to retain my perspective by recalling the details of that September in 2009. The month in which I experienced both a profound sense of loss and a profound sense of hope. A powerful lesson in a story that only a sunset of a sweet good-bye and the sunrise of a sweet beginning could tell.

# Loving Farrah

I was named after the blonde icon who defined the '70s. Farrah Fawcett was the fun-loving, free-spirited, Texas beauty who went from a toothpaste commercial to becoming the glamorous crime fighter in *Charlie's Angels*. In 1976, a poster of her posing as a Playboy centerfold in a red bathing suit became and still is the best selling pinup of all time, selling over twelve million copies. Her blond feathered hairstyle, known as "The Farrah," was embraced by anyone with access to a round-brush and blow-dryer. Farrah Fawcett defined an entire generation of women and practically paved the way for feminism armed with nothing but the latest fashions and a dazzling smile. For a namesake, that's quite a lot for a little Asian girl to live up to.

Growing up on a small farm in Cape Cod, I knew nothing of Farrah Fawcett's fame. The grandparents that raised me felt that the essentials were all that mattered, so Farrah Fawcett was buying sets of high-fashion boots in various colors and I was wearing my grandfather's flannel shirts and tying my grandmother's bandana around my head. The kids at school called me "Aunt Jemima." I didn't even own a hair-dryer until the late nineties. We barely had electricity! Instead, I wore my hair in two braids. Or, if I tried doing my hair at all, I did what my grandmother did, which was almost exactly like what I'd read about in the *Little House on the Prairie* books. We tied our hair in pin-curls, twisting it in a loop and tucking it in with a bobby pin until it air-dried. But my thick, black hair frizzed on the sides and stuck to my sweaty face in the humid New England summers. Trust me. I was better off in braids.

My acting career began much younger than Farrah Fawcett's. My first role was playing Goldilocks in the first grade. I know, I know. The irony was lost on me at the time, but I played the role with such vigor and conviction that the entire class was rolling with laughter when I fell though Baby Bear's chair. After that, I thought school would be easier. But the kids ran after me at recess, pulling at their eyes and asking, "Do you come from Chinaaaah?" and singing, "ding-dah-ding-ching-chang! Is that your language?" before running away, squealing with laughter. When we loaded up on the big yellow bus, the one other Asian kid in our school always sat in the front, clinging to his Curious George stuffed monkey. Everyone yelled at me, "Are you going to sit by GEORGE and have China babies?!? Do you LOVE George?!? Is he your husband?!?" I was mean to George by refusing to acknowledge him, the little Chinese boy in glasses who was such a social reject that even I was ashamed to be associated with him.

While Farrah made headlines for going bra-less, I was taunted mercilessly for needing a bra in the fourth grade. That was the year I grew a foot and towered over everyone in Mrs. Fetinecci's class. I felt like a monster at five feet three inches. In class photos, I was always in the back row with my eyes closed. In my imagination, I figured if I closed my eyes, no one would see me. I desperately ached for someone to reach out to me and be my friend, but I was a giant with long, frizzy hair and boobs. Every time I raised my hand, people would make fun of me, saying I was smart because I was born in China. I would argue that I wasn't. That my last name was Walker, I was born in New Jersey and, really, I wasn't that smart; I was just a very fast reader. That was the year I learned to sit in the back corner, keep my head down, my mouth shut and my sweaters baggy. One day, the boy who sat in front of me turned around and whispered, "It's okay. I wish I could read as good as you." I burned with embarrassment behind thick, plastic frame glasses.

I'd been subscribing to *Seventeen, YM* and *Vogue* for most of my adolescent life, and the only time I saw a picture that looked remotely like me was on a cereal box. She was probably about six years old and definitely not Chinese or Korean, but she was brown and she had black hair. I cut the box face off and put it on my door, telling my friends that it was my first acting gig when I was a kid. Later, I found a Bongo jeans ad where the model had long black hair and wore white, vintage sunglasses like mine. Her hair and glasses covered most of her face, the color of her skin was just like mine in the summertime. I photocopied the ad, told everyone that it was me in my former life as a model and gave it out as Valentine cards. *The Joy Luck Club* was the first movie I saw that had Asian actresses as main characters. As I watched the video with my Chinese friend, I sighed, "They're so pretty. I wish I looked like that." My friend looked at me like I just blew frogs out of my nose. "You DO look like that," she snorted. Disbelieving, I ran to the mirror to check. Somehow, I was kind of Asian, but not a pretty-Asian, like the graceful women with soft features and gentle voices in the movie. As my grandfather told me on the farm, when I complained about my wide shoulders, "You were built for hard labor." There was nothing delicate about me.

While I was at the peak of my adolescent awkward phase, Farrah Fawcett was nominated for both an Emmy and a Golden Globe, shining and smiling with golden-haired heartthrob Ryan O'Neal on her arm. Having a boy talk to me, let alone touch me, made my entire body prickle with sweat. But it was hardly an issue, not when there were plenty of pretty girls who wore makeup, used curling irons, and wore skintight, acid-washed Guess? jeans and not dark denim from the Salvation Army. Boys paid me no attention until Antoine de Larkin, homecoming king, water-polo team caption, lead in all the school plays, and school mascot asked me to prom. I was excited at first, but on prom night, I suddenly felt like I was being collected as one of his many conquests. It was like I was living out a teen movie where the art freak goes to prom with the most popular boy in school and it's all a big joke. Then Antoine explained that he'd had trouble with the ATM. I was mortified that I had to pay for our tickets and pictures. Somehow, I have a feeling Farrah Fawcett never had to pay for her dates with her golden boys.

After the Antoine de Larkin experience, I was careful to only go out with men who were actually interested in me and not just what they might have thought I represented. It was when they described me as "exotic" that I seethed the most. I refused to detail my ethnicity, finding it awkward to explain that my father was Chinese, but had abandoned me at birth and that my mother, adopted from Korea, had pretty much decided that parenting wasn't for her. I simply stated that I grew up with my grandparents and that my family was white. I was a Walker, through and through. And it was true. My tall, Rob Lowe-lookalike cousin scoffed when I told him how other kids treated me as if I was a Martian. "Farrah, you are the most American girl I know. You're like apple pie!" Even within my own family, the fact that I was Asian and different never seemed to register. My ethnicity was neither a liability nor something to be proud of. It was merely to be ignored. Except for when I caught a look at myself in a mirror. If I happened to see my reflection, I was usually surprised at what I saw. Was I really so short? I was so much darker than I thought. My eyes didn't look right. They were so small, I felt like I had to put half an inch of eyeliner on my lids just to get them to show up. I gave up wrestling with my wiry, tangled hair and cut it all off with my own scissors at home.

In college, I tried taking classes in Humanities of Asia and did miserably. It was humiliating to be the only Asian in my class and then do the poorest in the one arena my classmates were certain I would dominate. In a professional presentation of my resume for another class, I was criticized for not emphasizing my Chinese heritage. And when I explained I didn't speak or read Chinese and that my last name was "Walker," the criticisms came in harder, accusing me of foolishly trying to hide my ethnicity.

A few years later, a good friend that I secretly loved told to me about his dream woman. Then he turned to me and said, "Farrah, you are the perfect woman...if only you were blonde." My heart shriveled and melted like heated metal. I wish I could tell you I slapped him. Or laughed in his face at his absurd expectations. Or walked out on him after giving an eloquent speech on prejudice and racism and ignorance. But I didn't. I cringed and was furious with myself. How could I not be blonde? What was my problem? Why couldn't I be tall and thin and be a woman he wanted and admired? Why was I only good on the inside? Was there any way I could change his mind about that image of a Farrah Fawcett-like beach girl and switch it out for a short, dark girl who cuts her own hair and reads the thesaurus for fun? My roommate found the story hilarious and bought me an awful, cheap blond wig for Christmas. I tried it on. Part as a joke and part hoping it might actually look good. Since then, I've tried on multiple blond wigs, some are even called "The Farrah." Not one looks remotely flattering, though. In all the small deficits my personal appearance may have, not one can compare with how absolutely awful I look as a blonde.

I have finally given up on ever having "perfect hair" blown out in soft, feathery waves. In settling for letting my hair be completely wild and unmanageable, now strangers stop me to ask where I get my funky, wild hair cut. I have learned to wear SPF 50, but still got asked by an Egyptian man if I was from a tribe across the Nile, which is a pretty cool question to be asked. In Thailand, the native women would ask to touch my skin, telling me how beautiful it is. It's the same color as theirs, I explain, but they disagree. It seems that no one in the world is free from assuming someone else is prettier as a more perfect version of what we think we ought to be. And if there's no escaping that sentiment, than I guess I'll just accept what I do have and be glad to know I make the world's worst blonde.

"Life is the first gift,
love is the second, and
understanding the third."

MARGE PIERCY

# Finding Meaning

On a Sunday evening in March 2010, my college routine turned upside down. A simply worded text message changed my life. I rushed out of my rented single room by my school and closed the door behind the life I once knew.

My mind raced around the words, "Dad's in the hospital." Those four words echoed in my head as I drove down that long stretch of freeway towards my parents' house. It didn't cross my mind to grab a jacket or even to change my clothes. I left with only a t-shirt and track shorts on.

Minutes seemed like hours and miles seemed almost endless. It was that strange sensation of having things change so quickly that time comes to a screaming halt.

Somehow I found myself seated in the chaotic emergency room cradling my Cambodian mother in my arms. We both watched in horror when my Vietnamese father began to convulse on the hospital bed. He shook uncontrollably until he fell into a sonorous sleep. As he rested, I took his hand in mine. His warm skin smelled of orange chicken from the Chinese Food restaurant we owned; a smell that I have come to know as my father's scent after a hard day at work. I had always imagined the foul odor of illness or blood to be on the skin of critically admitted patients, but never the sweet aromas of delicious food on my father's skin. It was strange to think that only a few hours before this, my father had been working and joking around at the restaurant. And then, at closing time, he finished cleaning up with my mother and brother when his body became paralyzed. He was unable to express his last running thoughts; he began to have seizures in my mother's arms.

The evenings after my father's major stroke, I sat at his bedside in the sterile intensive care unit muttering in both Cambodian and Vietnamese my guilt. I should have been there for him instead of putting so much time and effort into living this alternative life as someone else. Those missed calls, those missed visits, and those miss opportunities to connect with my father added weight onto my shoulders.

I went into college thinking I should become someone else, someone better. Someone who was better connected with my father's heritage. All I had thought about during my first half of college was *how can I become this person?*

I had sat at the front of my Vietnamese classes thinking that I could absorb the Vietnamese culture in my veins. It required learning another language and adding another loop to my social circle. It did not come naturally to me as I had initially thought, however. The cultural cues that I would have learned as a child became difficult skills to memorize as an adult.

My father admired my ambitious drive to learn the Vietnamese culture, but he quickly realized how much of my life revolved around this. He had asked me to discontinue Vietnamese activities if it proved too difficult and time consuming, but I insisted on continuing. It was that private moment I shared with my father at the dinner table with a Vietnamese book that I truly loved. Depite the countless hours I spent trying to become Vietnamese American, that was never me.

If I had heeded my father's advice and not tried so hard getting to know my father's culture, I could have spent more time getting to know and be with *my father*. But as I held his warm hands in the ICU, I knew deep inside that he didn't care whether I had chosen a bowl of pho or BBQ steak with *tuk prahok*. He did not see a contest of which ethnic group was better or the need to have them coexist in separate categories. All he saw and all he needed from me all those years was my love, support, and sincerity. On my father's final day in the hospital, in his final hours alive on earth, that is exactly what I gave him.

"Falling in love is awfully simple, but falling out of love is simply awful."

UNKNOWN

# Falling for Love

Falling describes my worst nightmare: a sudden descent from a rocky
precipice, jolting me from a relaxed slumber into pandemonium. I
flail my arms and legs as if such wild gesticulations will grant me the
miraculous gift of flight. How does such a lucid dream that awakes
me so abruptly describe how we *fall* in love? If this is falling, then
why do we say people fall *out* of love?

Instead of defining "fall" as the accidental plummet into the
unknown, what if we use another definition to explore the sensation
of falling in or out of love: the season. I can now feel fall as a velour
blanket that prepares me for a crisp winter; a blanket tied to the
sun-soaked coattails of summer. Fall is supple and understated, but
it quietly radiates a warm, burnt orange glow. Fall is cyclical, as is
the nature of human relationships. Fall is a season that will come
and go, as do our lovers, friends, and acquaintances.

When we *fall in love*, it is as if we open the hallway closet, and,
standing on our tiptoes, scour the top shelf for a comforter, duvet,
or plain old blanket. It is our favorite piece of material, that which
our bodies yearn to be wrapped with. It envelops us with the kind
of affection that looks, smells, and feels oh-so-familiar. Memories of
wrapping ourselves like a burrito in this Blanket of Love are tender,

kind, and sincere. When we fall into love's blanket, we feel so fortunate and blessed to remember its feeling. Love adorns our physical, mental, and spiritual cores once more.

But fall is predictable. Winter will follow. The kindhearted, compassionate affection we draped ourselves with when we fell in love may be tousled with the advent of winter. Perhaps the seams of integrity begin to unravel, or the blanket becomes riddled with holes where genuine intentions once held it intact. Maybe we sew patches over these holes, meaning to forget these truths, but, in actuality, they are poorly constructed band-aids, disguised as solutions. Perhaps the strength of the blanket is tested when unforeseen life events unfold. The blanket may have doubled as a pile of tissues, doused with salty tears after the gravity of a break-up has settled in. This is how winter rears its ugly head. Winter rattles our core, lifts the gossamer curtain on the delusion that we thought was love, and forces us to take a good, long, self-prescribed examination of ourselves.

When we *fall out of love*, it is as if our Blanket of Love could not withstand winter's storm. The blanket lays disheveled at our feet. But I do not think this rumpled, worn out blanket is meant to be thrown at the wayside. We can wash it, fold it, and return it to the safe haven of our closet. Or, we can shake out its wrinkles, embrace it, then choose to do something else with it.

There is a children's story that describes how a boy's classmates taunt him relentlessly for bringing a safety blanket to school. His clever mother decides to snip a piece of it for the boy to store in his pocket. This small piece brings him comfort and happiness. He has an instant, personal, portable reminder of safety at all times.

Instead of storing my Blanket of Love away after the winter storms have calmed, I have made the choice to keep love conscious and tangible. I have decided to carry a corner of love in my own pocket, so that I am also ready to grab the well-worn patch with lint and all, at any time. It will help remind me that love is not meant to be shelved.

I am grateful that I have fallen into and out of love, so that I could learn to reach into my pocket, smooth this small piece of blanket with the tips of my fingers, and infuse love into relationships with my next lover, future friends, and new acquaintances. I want to emanate love in light of fall's burnt orange glow and winter's tattered truths.

Falling into the cycle of being in love and being out of love assures me that love really does make "the world go 'round." And I am going to spread every last bit of fluffy tenderness from my own little corner of love, as I continue to marvel at the world's steadfast spin.

"What is patriotism but the love
of the food one ate as a child?"

LIN YUTANG

# Leggo My Eggo

When I was in kindergarten, I didn't like standing out. But I couldn't do anything about the shape of my eyes, my dark, thick, straight hair, or my foreign-sounding last name. I could, however, try to fit in other ways. My parents didn't know much about American culture, but thankfully I had another guide. Television. It was like an encyclopedia to me, an index to understanding how their culture worked and what was considered "normal." TV was my direct connection to manners, slang, clothes, and especially food.

My mother was pretty good about letting me try different American foods when we had enough money. One day, a commercial for Eggo Waffles came on the TV. I watched with interest as the kids dropped a round piece of bread into the toaster. It kind of looked like the Wonder Bread my mom would toast for me every morning for breakfast, only it was yellow and covered in square patterns. And instead of putting a little butter and Maggi Seasoning soy sauce on it, the kids in the commercial poured a strange dark sauce over theirs. As soon as it popped out of the toaster, they'd yell, "Leggo my Eggo!" All I could think was, "I want to try this!" I thought it would be so cool to whip out some Eggo Waffles next time a friend was over to play.

When the commercial came on again, I ran and called my mother to show her what I wanted. We both sat in front of the TV and studied the Eggo Waffle box. When the day came to go to the market, I knew exactly what to look for. My mother and I walked the aisles but couldn't find it because we didn't realize it was a frozen breakfast item. Soon a store clerk came to our rescue. "I'm looking for Eggo Waffles!" I said hopefully. And he directed us to the frozen foods aisle.

Seeing Mom grab the big yellow box and place it in the shopping cart, I could barely contain my joy, jumping up and down the aisle and skipping all the way to the checkout counter. I couldn't wait to try one when I got home, even if it was supposed to be served in the morning. *But why wait for breakfast when heaven is near?*

When I got home, I looked at the picture instructions and popped two waffles into the toaster. That was easy. It was like toasting bread, which I already knew how to do. While they were toasting, I realized that I'd forgotten to ask the clerk about the dark sauce that went over the waffles. That's okay, I thought. I'd just search the pantry for something that might work. I wasn't sure about a lot of the sauces my mom had stashed. There were so many to choose from and I didn't want to experiment with every bottle. Besides, I only had six packages of the waffles and I didn't want to waste them. After thinking about it for a few minutes, I went with what I knew and that was the Maggi Sauce. I thought, "This is it!" I use it on my scrambled eggs, white rice and even my toast. It's so delicious on everything I put it on; this *must be* the dark sauce they pour over the waffles. I was impressed with myself that I already had a foot into this American food culture thing.

I was salivating when the waffles popped out of the toaster, just like in the commercial. The only that was missing was someone to say, "Leggo my Eggo!"

I carefully placed the warm waffles on the plate and smelled the sweet bread. I remembered that in the commercial, the sauce drizzled over the waffle, flowing over its edges and falling onto the plate. But when I poured the Maggi Sauce over the square indented pockets on the bread, it soaked right through the waffle and disappeared along the lines where I'd poured it. I crinkled my nose and tilted my head in curiosity, wondering "what happened?" But I shrugged it off within five seconds. I was finally going to taste my first American waffle—and that's what mattered!

When I bit into the waffle, it was so sweet yet so salty too. I thought it was a weird combination. I wanted to analyze it a bit more, so I took another bite. It wasn't as bad as I thought. It was sweet on the first bite and then the saltiness came right after. I never experienced that kind of flavor before. But the kids on TV loved the Eggo Waffles so much. In the commercial, they fought over who got to eat the next waffle, yet I had to force myself to finish mine with a crooked smile. My mouth was so confused with the taste. However, I told myself that if I wanted to be a part of the American culture, I had to eat it. Besides, my mother would have been furious if I had wasted my parents' hard-earned money. It took me a whole month to finally polish off the whole box of Eggo Waffles.

Despite this little snag, I still depended on TV to learn about American culture. I was still curious how Americans dressed, what music they listened to, what slang terms they used and what interesting foods they ate. I studied every commercial and show I saw on TV. I wanted to be an American so badly.

Then one day, one particular advertisement caught my eye. It featured a woman on a dark brown bottle. She was talking to a little girl who had a stack of pancakes, telling her, "My syrup is thick, rich and yummy." Then the commercial zoomed to the stack of pancakes. It showed the thick, gooey sauce being poured over the pancakes and over the edges like in the "Leggo Waffle" commercial! I was so excited. My eyes widened with glee. I felt like I'd found out the answer to "Who did it?" in "Clue"! I was so proud of myself; I was beaming. I was eager to meet "Mrs. Butterworth" and see what all the fuss was about!

When I finally tried the waffles with the syrup, the way Americans eat them, I instantly understood why the children in the commercial were so excited. I shook my head up and down and felt the gratification of finally understanding another American food item. And you bet that if someone else wanted to steal my waffles, I would shout out, "Leggo my Eggo!"

# aperitif / a bottle of you

TRACI KATO-KIRIYAMA

when you are least looking,
i will take a sip of your breath,
make note of the hops and petals
swirling on the back of my deft palate,
and create a new concoction that i
can sell to the bar down at the corner
i won't make a million dollars, but
i will drive the tenders to chalk this up,
charge ten crowns and 2,000 yen and
the people will pay, will come in droves
for a spell beyond their first dram, far too
happy drunk to discuss what made them
exchange all the dollar bills they usually
reserve for cab rides and cheap tips, just to
spend a moment with what i cured of you in a
bottle of enchantment bitters and ecstasy rum

# Can't Hurry Love

Everyone has a story. A love story.

Being a hopeless romantic growing up, I have always looked for love that makes you totally feverish and giddy beyond words and kisses. And now as a single independent mom, love is what feels right for the heart.

It has been five years since my divorce, and while it was a time of heartache and uncertainty, I have decided to be the best single mom and focus on the things that I want to pursue like business development in the entertainment industry and writing. I call this loving myself. That means that I will be the only one responsible for my actions and decisions.

I have been troubled by the fact that I am being pressured to go out on a date and open myself to the possibility of having a boyfriend by close friends and family members. Personally, I believe that somewhere at the right time and place, love will find me.

Sure I still have a list of my Prince Charming qualities. Is he tall enough, brainy, laughs a lot and financially stable? Does he like to travel? Is he going places? The list goes on and on. I still fantasize how my Prince Charming will sweep me off my feet, the type who will support and challenge me mentally.

*I know what I want.* I have carved a life that is productive, fulfilling and exciting and have given myself a pat on the back for my so-called bravery of being alone. I will not give up years of hard work to fall in love with Mr. Wrong. And when I find Mr. Right, I will compromise my time without sacrificing my career. I have become an independent career-oriented single mom.

The past five years have been growing-up years for me. It has been a conscious effort to make wise use of my time and only recently that I have made a conscious attempt to stretch the potential of my love life and take baby steps outside my comfort zone. The awakening came when my sons, fourteen year-old Franco and my eleven year-old Inigo, gave me their blessing to go out on dates and I realized how I had this desire to get out there and conquer.

You open yourself again and embrace what you are given. Then you find yourself in situation you never knew could exist for you. You find real freedom to love. I was tired of being scared of falling in love. But time and forgiveness have taught me to open myself to sweet possibilities. If I find someone and there is magic, then I will proceed. Still, pains of a broken marriage prompt me to question myself, "Again, what was I thinking?"

Ah, love… makes the world go round, doesn't it? For without it, I find no other reason that even equals this for anyone to want to live. Life is hard as it is, and without love that would be one dull, sad existence!

Unfortunately, as the quote says, "The course of true love never did run smooth." Such words can't be any truer. Any relationship is difficult because we have two different individuals coming together with their own sets of personalities, thoughts, opinions, and principles that make them their own unique persons—then you add to that equation outside factors.

Smooth sailing is definitely out. Yet, despite that truth, why do we forge on and get into relationships? It is simply because there is no other greater feeling in the world—a true natural high. As I said, love makes the world go round.

I am now doing an act of courage, a leap of faith in love combined with constant knocking on heaven's doors to send me Prince Charming.

I like where I am today. I have two great sons and amazing family and friends. I have a wonderful job and I am writing.

I am finally living entirely in the present. Someday, love will find a way. That makes for a thought that never fails to bring peace in my heart.

"In the midst of winter, I found there was within me an invincible summer."

ALBERT CAREB

# Left Hand Turn

Three years ago I burned my hand. My painting hand. Severely. A "de-gloving" they called it. With all that skin hanging off I was happy to get the morphine in my system. I am glad my friend Lynn was there to get me to the hospital.

Every morning after the necessary skin scraping and the "de-breeding" in the hydra bath tank, I was happy the therapists granted my wish of letting me sit in warm water and take in the sun pouring into the frosted cage window above me. I knew they had other patients, I didn't want to overindulge, but the few extra minutes in the embryonic safety of the room, even after the aching skin scraps, gave me back my breath. More peace than the six packs of opiate sticks in the IV. I talked with the nurse and the orderly about hardship and goodness. About the value of people trying to help you though in life, and the clarity of being able to recognize it.

In my mind's eye a camera flash illuminates a large dark room, and for a brief moment, I am allowed to see in that quicksilver light the faces of all those friends gathered for me. In a glimpse it's gone again, but I have the good fortune of having that memory burned in my mind forever.

It's left me for a different need than when I was a child. I now had to paint stories. That deep yearning made me pack my Chevy van and drive into an unknown. I still see the lone figure in the back lane in my rearview mirror. The stance of an immigrant who knew the way. My dad helped me build a bed in that van, with a false cabinet under which would conceal my portfolio from those testy border guys at the 49th parallel. I don't think it was my dad's most beautiful work, but it might have been his most important. I think he might have even relished getting one more over on a guy with an official brown shirt.

I can recall the ease in Dad's breath when I called home from the first bar in the Montana frontier.

My brothers and I still have a warm laugh for that mustard seed faith. They had a calling as well, both becoming ministers. Seemed they had just as long a road; it was just paved with bricks made up of semesters at some seminary.

I liked my road, that road as wide and dusty and lonesome as I could embrace, all those summer heat waves searing off the Montana pavement. For a moment you're the only one standing on the white line on that grey highway. I can think of lone dogs and Springsteen and earlier family road trips in the Rocket Olds 88, when we could still as a family grab some sleep at a dew sprinkled rest area in the night open sky. I had a message too; I just didn't know what it was.

## Truth or Consequences

Somewhere near Truth or Consequences. I'm in New Mexico, and I'm tired of the interstate's four-lane melancholy. I long for an old thin highway, one I can share the intimacy of the local rolling terrain and string of phone poles with. I still like the look and feel and smell of creosol of those poles, ever since playing in the abandoned tar plant across the tracks from home. That old riveted, tank-filled, black and rusted landscape was my Disneyland. The security guard was certainly goofy. And on weekends we could lift the large Styrofoam blocks over the fence from the adjoining factory, which provided rafts we could steer right through the black sludge to new fields afar. We were large ferrymen on the petroleum-filled river Hades.

I'm reeled back in from this memory by red flashing lights irritating my altogether tired eyes. I didn't know until months later about drug dealers and vans with strange plates and "wetbacks" in the area. That sheriff pulled me over. In his midnight he had to draw his gun and make me "stand over there on the curb." I am still looking around trying to find a curb in that episode. Nothing but dying sage and desert darkness. That cop was probably as scared as I was. Maybe he'd never even seen a Canadian, let alone one driving barefoot and road beaten though his darkness. Can't wait to get to California now. The desert has become just that.

"A man travels the world over
in search of what he needs
and returns home to find it."

GEORGE MOORE

# Heartland

As a child, I sometimes questioned the decision of my parents to settle in this unassuming part of the country. Just before the Vietnam War began, the Tejadas were one of a handful of Oriental families living in Lawton, a small city in Southwest Oklahoma near the Texas border.

"The pace of life reminded us of our province in the Philippines," my mother told me. "The cost of living is affordable and we could live as we did back home." Despite his assignments around the globe, my father never wanted to leave.

This scale of life was manageable for my parents. Two of the other Oriental families we knew were fellow Filipinos. Auntie Euphemia and Uncle Candido Merza had five children of whom Rosalie, the youngest, was our age. Rosalie was allowed to be a free spirit who dabbled in artistic pursuits like ceramics. In the Campos family, Mary Ann, Rose Marie, Bobby and Eddy were all in our age group; Uncle Felix and Auntie Elma came from the same part of the Philippines as my parents—the Visayan Islands—where our fathers knew each other as young men. Needless to say, our families became particularly close. Later, two Guamanian families, the Indelacios and the Quengas, would join us. Our fathers were soldiers in the U.S. Army, the common denominator in our circle.

The only Oriental store in town was operated out of a house on the main street to the local airport, and would be moved when the owner relocated to another neighborhood. The limited inventory consisted mainly of bottled seasonings and dried foods. I remember the soft candies wrapped in rice paper that melted in the mouth and the sensation of biting into honey puff balls, special treats my mother would buy for us while we waited patiently outside on the steps as she purchased groceries. Hatsuko, a Japanese woman married to an American soldier, owned the store. My younger sister was Hatsuko's favorite—she would always tell her to take a handful of Japanese crackers from the large tin near the cash register. There was no Oriental restaurant; on occasion Hatsuko would offer to cook some Japanese food we could buy.

Eating out mostly meant visiting each other's homes and barbecuing marinated steaks, pork ribs and chicken wings. For special occasions, there would be traditional foods prepared by our mothers, including *siopao*, a steamed bun with a savory meat filling and wedges of hard-boiled egg; *lumpia*, our light and tasty rendition of an eggroll; *pancit*, noodles with assorted meats and vegetables; *ensaymada*, an airy version of a French *brioche* with cheese grated on top; and homemade pickles made from papayas and mangoes. Our families would plant fertile gardens and grow the vegetables used in cooking daily meals. Mommy and Auntie Euphemia often shared the long beans, bitter melons and leafy vegetables they regularly harvested.

My sisters and I spent our formative years in a place where children were raised to be respectful. Families attended church on Sundays and ate dinner together each evening. A person's word was his or her bond.

Unlike many new immigrants to America, we did not experience life in busy and crowded cities on the East Coast or West Coast, as did my husband. We were referred to as Orientals until the late 1970s, when we became Asians. There was no Chinatown or Asian District where my family could shop and eat our traditional dishes, or mingle daily among others of our own familiar race and ethnicity. There is power in numbers, and as a child I had no exposure to Asians in public office, in the media, or as literary authors and artists. Rather, I was acutely aware of how different my upbringing was from my friends. I was the good student who was not permitted to participate in accepted rites of passage, such as attending sleepovers with girlfriends or going on dates. What could have been a culture clash instead became a discerning balancing act between incorporating my identity as a traditionally-raised Filipina with navigating my way in a society that pushed me to be expressive and independent.

If I ever felt deprived of a sense of belonging, of what I then considered to be the definitive Asian experience in America, there were consolations. The traits of industriousness and scholarship my mother inculcated soon made it possible for me to expand my boundaries. I was offered admission to Ivy League universities on the East Coast, as were my sisters. Independently, I traveled around the world and lived in other regions of the country. Eventually, my husband and I returned to my hometown where I would write my books, flooded by recollections of my family, friends and long ago self each time I encountered a familiar landmark.

While I had roamed far afield as an adult, time and progress had changed my childhood home. Lawton has now been anointed by the national media as the epicenter of the new American heartland, a microcosm of the entire country. Filipinos are the single largest ethnic community, joined by a diverse population represented by Koreans, South Asian Indians, Mexicans, Native Americans, Germans, Africans, Lebanese and Caribbeans with restaurants, stores, and communities that cater to these cultures. The army post is well-established as one of the major military installations in the country. Native Americans are major employers who own and operate a number of casinos. A cultural benchmark was achieved when the local television station began featuring anchors and reporters of Asian, Native American, Hispanic and African-American ancestry.

In retrospect, my parents were pioneers and visionaries. In their wisdom, they had staked their claim and settled far from their native land with the intention of making a home for their young family—a tolerant and protected space where we could thrive, rooted in our heritage and traditions. The sense of community and friendship they experienced in the Southwest reminded them of their homeland, and my parents in turn helped build a vibrant and diverse city that welcomed other immigrants to this part of the world. This is the reason why, after turns in broadcasting, government and education, I decided to remain where my parents bought their first home.

When most people speak of the heartland, what emerges is an outmoded vision of Middle America in the mid-20th century. But to me, the concept of a heartland encompasses the notion of home. Southwest Oklahoma is my family's home and truly where my heart is.

# In a Better Place

When I was fifteen years old, my brother Kenny committed suicide. I have four older brothers: Bryan, Huan, Kenny, and Tommy. When we were younger, Bryan took me shopping, Huan locked me in my parents' closet, Tommy took me to the movies, and Kenny attempted to cut my hair. My childhood memories were of my brothers and me laughing, playing, and loving each other.

The afternoon of August 10, 2007, Tommy was in the living room working on his laptop and I was in my parent's room watching shows on the computer. Tommy's phone rang and he ran out the door. Puzzled, I walked outside and saw his papers, books, and laptop still on the table. I didn't think much of it at first, until my mother came home from work two hours earlier than usual. When I walked into the kitchen to greet her, she looked as if she'd wanted to cry but was too numb to do so. My stomach went sour and I wondered if she found my report card from last semester. "Hey Ma, are you okay?" I asked.

My mother stopped chopping vegetables, taking my wrist in her hand. "Kenny is going to kill himself. He wrote an email to your sister-in-law Yen. Yen called your brothers. They're all trying to find him. You do not tell your father, you understand?" She continued cooking dinner for my father.

My heart dropped; my body felt numb, cold, and lifeless. Somehow, I managed to walk to my room. I called Kenny's cell phone but his inbox was full. As tears welled up in my eyes, I kept dialing his number just to hear his voice. After five long minutes, I asked my friend for a ride. "Ron, I really need you to pick me up. I can't explain, can you just please come for me?" He was confused but agreed. As I was putting on my jeans, all these thoughts rushed to my head about Kenny. He was the closest to me out of all my brothers. If I had a problem or was bored and wanted to talk, I would call him, his phone number was the only number I had memorized. No matter what the situation was, he was there in a heartbeat. He listened to me and showed his love to me in strange and wonderful ways.

Before I knew it, Ron was calling me to come outside. I walked out to his car and looked at him. I didn't say a word; I just sat and stared out the window. "Tina, are you okay?" he asked.

"Just drive." He didn't know where to go so he ended up driving to his house.

He asked me again, "Tina, are you okay?"

I cried and like my tears, the words came flooding out: "My brother's going to commit suicide and there's nothing I can do. What am I suppose to do, Ron?! I know nothing! My mother isn't telling my father. I don't understand! I am confused; I am angry. He needs to be okay... Kenny needs to be okay, Ron."

My friend's mouth dropped. "I am so sorry Tina, I really don't know what to tell you. It'll be okay." He thought watching a movie would get my mind off of things, so he put on a Jim Carry one. Instead of enjoying the movie, all I could think about was how Kenny was going to take his life away. Is *he going to jump in the ocean? Take a knife and stab himself? What in the world is going to happen? Is this really happening? Why is he doing this?* I just saw him a few weeks ago and though I could tell being separated from his wife was taking a toll, I would never have guessed he was depressed enough to kill himself.

"Everything is going to be okay Tina. He'll be okay. I'm here for you," Ron said before I opened the car door. I nodded. As I walked to my doorstep, I took deep breaths and closed my eyes. My parents were sleeping and Tommy wasn't home. I couldn't believe that anyone could sleep at a time like this. But then I wasn't sure that my father even knew. I wondered whether Tommy had found Kenny. I got ready for bed and asked myself, what is going to happen now? Lying on my bed, my mind filled with memories of Kenny, from our fights about my math homework to our talks about how I'd be the first female president of our country. I finally fell asleep around five in the morning but that sleep ended shortly.

I woke up to my father screaming "Where is my son? What do you mean he's dead? How could you hide this from me? He's my son. Where is he? What is going on? How could this happen? Where is my son?!" I walked outside to see my father's face pale pacing back and forth with his hands holding his head, my mother sitting on the coach softly weeping, finally my brothers one by one showing up with teary eyes.

I went to the bathroom, crawled into a ball and cried, saying, "Why did you do this, Kenny? Are you happy? Is this what you want?" Though I felt angry and frustrated, I somehow pulled myself up and got ready for the day.

Family and friends came over every hour throughout the day. Meggie, who was Huan's girlfriend at the time, was the only person I could talk to. I cried to her, telling her how I didn't understand. Meggie broke it down to me and told me what happened. Huan and she went to different motels with Kenny's photo, asking the mangers if they'd seen him. Tommy checked anywhere he could, and Yen went to their favorite places and asked people. They did everything they could.

The police found Kenny at a Motel 6 in Westminster. They said he was in a suit, his hands crossed over his chest. The room was clean and peaceful. On the nightstand, they found a bottle of Corona, a pill, and *The Peaceful Pill Handbook*.

Finally, my brothers, parents, and sisters-in-law went to station to identify the body. My parents said I was too young to come. They were afraid I couldn't handle the reality of my brother's death. When everything was said and done, it was indeed Kenny's body. So the funeral process began.

My family is Buddhist but Yen and her family are Catholic. As if it couldn't get any worse, my father refused to have a Catholic funeral. Finally everybody agreed to have both a Buddhist and Catholic funeral.

The day of Kenny's funeral was eventful. Hours of being my knees bowing and praying to guide Kenny to his new life took the life out of me. I was on my knees when they brought his body out. My uncle and aunt came to my family repeating, "Do not cry, he's in a better place, do not cry, it'll be okay. Do not cry, you cannot be weak. Show strength." The room temperature dropped; it became cold and my body felt like it was being pushed down. I crumbled and cried so hard I couldn't breathe. I watched my brother being put in a coffin so my family could put him in peace. When I came up to see him, I touched his chest and cried. "I hope you'll find your way, Kenny."

My mother came over and fixed his tie. "Don't be afraid to touch him, Tina. He'll be in peace now. He's starting his new life." I looked at his cold lifeless body and walked away.

When it was time to cremate him I'd already shed enough tears. I felt numb when the workers put Kenny's coffin in the oven.

Once it was done, I walked outside and saw a yellow butterfly. It was fluttering around my family and landed on my father's shoulders. "Look, it's Kenny!" Meggie said. I didn't think much of it until the butterfly got closer to my face then flew away. We went home to rest and once we got out of the car, the butterfly was there. It flew around us one last time before flying away for good.

"He's in a better place now," my mother told me and walked inside the house. I remember standing outside, closing my eyes and taking a deep breath as I told myself, "Yes, Kenny is in a better place."

# Secrets of a Chihuahua Mom

*It's funny. I have always been an open book—a journal left to blow around in the wind. That's what being a mom can do to you. You lose track of yourself while you are breastfeeding, baby proofing and teaching respect and manners. No, it doesn't happen by choice. One day you just wake up and wonder what happened...*

Every Tuesday I take baby Julia to play with Thomas the Train at our local book store. One Tuesday, while I was sitting on the floor of the kiddie section, a red-haired boy dressed in a t-shirt with faux tuxedo piping and a pair of jeans with a hole above his left knee casually sauntered by. He stopped, cocked his head, looked me in the eye and then for the next half hour he animatedly shared his wild tales of being five—his kid sister's quirks, info on the largest T-Rex ever found and why he thought broccoli should be outlawed.

That afternoon, when my six year-old came home from school, I asked her about *her* story:

"Madison, do you know where you were born?"

"Florida," she replied matter-of-factly. "In the hospital at 11:51 pm."

Well that was easy. Maybe she had already secretly written her story.

But then she suddenly stopped playing Wii and asked, "So...where were *you* born?"

I wasn't expecting her question. I paused for a moment and replied, "Korea."

She left and then re-appeared a minute later. "Where's Korea?" She was carrying the globe from the den and was pointing at it for me to show her.

I found Seoul, showed her the outline of the country and said, "I was adopted when I was about Julia's age."

She had a blank look on her face. "What's 'adopted' mean?"

"Well...Grandma saw me when I was living in a very special home and she chose me to be her family."

"Like when we got Roxy and Ella!" Her eyes were wide with excitement.

I smiled. "Exactly!"

Madison went back to conquering Sims Kingdom and I was left to ponder our conversation. So it stood. In my daughter's eyes, my legacy was comparable to a Chihuahua.

Kids are amazing. They will scream at you, make you tear your hair out of your head and drive you to lose your mind. And, in a split-second, they will change your life. I had always been a dog-lover, but now I definitely needed a better story. After all, stories are how people connect, how we network and most importantly, how our children grow up and learn the significance of their own stories. No, I wasn't ready for my story to go to the dogs!

The thing is, even though I didn't know where I was born or who I was born to, I don't remember asking about Korea or my birth parents. I didn't know any world other than my adopted mom—my real mom. She pushed uniqueness and individuality, and I bought into it. Yes, anything to account for the fact that I was the only girl with slanted eyes... and a tan.

Throughout life I was introduced to different cultures and religions—I grew up eating *empanadas* and mini pizzas from street cart vendors in Central America, and we always visited our Italian relatives in St. Petersburg who bickered over holiday meals. I was raised Roman

Catholic, broke *challah* and danced the *Hora* at Jewish summer camp, and at twenty-something I almost married a Conservative Baptist. But no, I never remembered hanging out in Korea-Town, contemplating Buddhism or celebrating Korean culture long-term.

Why not?

According to Wikipedia, I am one of the .5% of Korean Americans that populate the U.S., and given the numerous cities I have lived in, Wackipedia (as Madison calls it) is right on target. Looking back, I could count the Asians in class, on the block or at work—that's right... one. Ding! Did I win a prize? Um...yes. Individuality.

The problem was, when I broke out on my own, I was so wrapped up in being unique that I was uncomfortable competing to conform to Asiatic stereotypes. (That's my story and I'm sticking to it.) To date, I can't do math faster than drying cement and steamed rice swirls me into a relentless carb coma. In college I balked at the thought of joining the Asian Club... because really... was I Asian? Um... no.

I am still the most Caucasian Asian most people know. I'm not being ignorant or insensitive. I'm being real. Growing up in a Caucasian family *is* different than growing up in an Asian one. First-generation Asians shake their heads when I tell them I don't know how to make stir fried noodles or steamed tofu...or when I try to turn the tables and impress them with my meatloaf-making abilities. I don't blame them. The meatloaf isn't that great.

So this year, for my fortieth birthday, I decided to join my friends and family for my first Korean BBQ. My friend's husband, who was Irish American had been stationed in Korea when he was in the military and he guided us through the delicacies and the main course. The red coals crackled, the meat sizzled and we all laughed at the irony of the situation.

As I sat watching my family, their eyes filled with excitement and wonder, time seemed to stand still. In that moment, I realized that being Asian American meant that I was fortunate to have two great worlds in the palm of my hands — Eastern and Western — and I finally understood my legacy.

Today, learning how to combine, preserve and pass down both cultures means twice the responsibility. It doesn't matter what I didn't know, it only matters that I persevere *to* know. And not only for myself, for my girls as well. We are a culmination of all of our experiences. The way I look at it, I've been "one up" on bacon and eggs, now I just need to even the score and concentrate on *bulgogi*.

# The Stitch

One month after the wedding, I came home to a UPS box placed on my dresser. It was addressed from Ms. Peg Olson. Upon reading her name, I immediately opened the box with my husband beside me.

A tear shed after reading the first paragraph of the letter:

*Dear Tam,*

*Although this gift is arriving a little late, I must tell you that I felt it was important to send a knitted present. When I knit something, I think about the person or people for whom I am knitting with every stitch. There are thousands of stitches in this table runner and indeed, I did think about you and your family with every stitch.*

In the box, I found the table runner and a copy of the *Livonia Observer* dated Thursday, December 4th, 1980. Glancing over the headlines throughout the newspaper, I found it remarkable that many of the same concerns appear in papers today. *Schools to Sue Over Stingy State Aid Plan* was on the front page along with *Students Seek Aid for Refugee Camp* and a picture of my family below it.

Looking at the portrait, I was reminded of what took place ten months before my parents' arrival in Michigan. They left Vietnam on January 13th, 1980 to escape from Communism and in pursuit of freedom. On their journey to Thailand, their rickety boat narrowly survived an onslaught of heavy currents and thunderstorms. Even worse, the pirates from Thailand ransacked their boat, taking all of the women and leaving the men and children behind. Thankfully, they left my mother alone since she was pregnant with me, but she had to watch the other women in pain. A week later, the pirates returned the women back to their families, only to discover that all of the children had passed away. In quiet tears and embrace, my parents mourned the loss of their first-born son and nephew.

Once my parents arrived to the processing center in Thailand, they were scheduled to be transferred to the refugee camp in Songhkla. Australia, France, Germany, and Italy admitted those who had family residing in the country. America was the only country taking in refugees with no relatives. Those who fell in this category were sent to the same camp as my parents.

For the following months, each day mirrored itself with moments of eating and anticipating news of acceptance. Traveling in the same journey and living together created a sense of camaraderie amongst the refugees. Empathy allowed for them to deepen their relationships as they shared stories of their family in Vietnam and the ones lost along the way. Evenings would be filled with conversations about their dreams and how they look forward to a life with peace and simplicity. All of them chose to live from a stance of hope.

During my parents' stay in Songkhla, my mother knitted sweaters for other refugees in the camp as a source of income. As for my father, he studied and practiced English in preparation for our move to America. In June, my parents welcomed my arrival and named me "Tam," which means "compassion" in Vietnamese. They paired it with a middle name in dedication of my late older brother and together, the name "Minh Tam" means "pure soul."

A few weeks after I was born, my family received notice from the processing center that our paperwork had been misplaced. We were asked to relocate to Indonesia for further news of resettlement to America. Upon arriving to our next location, we were stationed at one of the barracks in Galang Island, where we were assigned a bunk bed with another family above us. My father continued to learn English and fetched water from the well on a daily basis. To make sure they had milk for me, my mother used the money she earned from knitting and bought bread to sell it to the rest of the refugees in the camp every morning.

The boredom and uncertainty of camp life created an undertone of unhappiness. At complete surrender, the speaker announced those who had received any letters and the names of people accepted for resettlement each day. For over three months, my parents experienced a whirlwind of emotions only to hear in October, "Vu Duc Hung... family of three." Immediately after the announcement, my father rushed to the office to confirm the call and verify the documents. At last, the waiting was over but my parents felt waves of sadness and uncertainty. They knew soon we would start our new life in a foreign land, unsure about the future, while leaving our friends behind. We were told of our destination and departure date: Michigan the weekend after Thanksgiving.

Upon arrival, our sponsors greeted us by the gate. The six months of planning and waiting had finally ended and the next challenge was finding a home for our family in Michigan. They worked together to find a place in the general area because of the two tentative job offers for my father. One was at the Plymouth Hilton Hotel and the other was custodial work with Livonia Public Schools. There was also a posting on the newspaper asking for clothing and donations to help cover living and medical expenses until we were adjusted. A handful of students from Franklin High School and their advisors, Ms. Peg Olson and Mr. John Rennels, came to our aid. Their generosity in time and effort has left my family in a debt of gratitude.

Before we were able to situate in a place of our own, Ms. Olson and her son, Matt, welcomed us into their home. They immersed my family into the American culture by exposing us to the food and customs. From Ms. Olson, we grew a liking for sloppy joes and donuts. We also learned common courtesy phrases such as "thank you" and "please." As for Mr. Rennels, he stopped by every morning to teach my father how to drive. Following each lesson, my parents took classes to learn English. Within a few weeks, my family felt a sense of community in Northville, Michigan.

After two cold winters, my mother and father were convinced to move to a warmer climate. In January of 1982, my family left to start a new beginning in California. We kept in touch with Mr. Rennels and Ms. Olson throughout the years by calling each other and writing letters. Over twenty years later, I took a trip to Michigan and reconnected with the both of them and their families in person.

As I look around at my family each time we gather, I often think about the love and generosity given to us from the students of Franklin High School, Mr. Rennels, Ms. Olson, and my parents. Through their actions, my brothers and I were given the opportunity to pursue our passion for service and most importantly, they gave us the freedom to create our own lives. Each word woven into this story is a dedication to their kindness. Their love gives meaning and depth to this world by being examples of what it means to be life giving. They gave generously without expectation.

The journey my parents took upon themselves taught me a valuable lesson. Up until this day, they always mention about the wonderful people they met in Michigan. Although their experiences were difficult in Thailand, it was hardly discussed or a focus of our conversations growing up. My parents wanted to engrain with us the good things that came out of it and how kind and welcoming this world can be. They wanted us to live a life of gratitude and how a situation can be looked at differently by the way we position our lens. It is what we learn and take action that matters in this lifetime.

# I Am. Thou Art. I Am Art.

Sitting in L.A. traffic on the cusp of a summer sunset, I look up at the boundless pink and orange sky. *Little ole' me on this vast Earth, within the immeasurable universe.* A hidden pocket of thoughts unleashes, and thus the contemplation begins.

Organized tumult. Exuberant terror. Timid passion. That's my best attempt at describing the paradox of the first decade of adulthood; the journey to discover the self in the context of relationships, career, and life's purpose.

As I push the gas pedal ever so gently to close the three-foot gap that opened up in the past ten minutes, a teardrop unsuspectingly falls. *What am I doing?* says the girl who aced all but one math class in her sixteen years of schooling, who co-founded this non-profit organization and attended that political conference, who pulled all-nighters on Friday nights to make room for a second internship. Such was the guaranteed path to success and stability. Such was convention. This girl in the reflection of my side view mirror has religiously followed that path, fighting her passion for acting, dance, and film every painstaking step of the way.

It's an appropriate time to begin my impassioned lash against society and its expectations. However, the only person I can genuinely point fingers at is myself. I got lost in my perception of success: title and stability. I witnessed theater and dance major graduates wait tables until some eventually "got realistic" and found office jobs. Those who stuck to it constantly struggled with money. I was a coward; I wanted the easy way out. I was the one who told myself that I could never make it as an artist.

Now let's add the Chinese immigrant factor to this epic internal battle: My single mother gave up *everything* to bring me to America. She gave me opportunities she never even dreamed of as a child of the Cultural Revolution in China. How can I possibly trade in engineer-investment banker-doctor for actor-dancer-starving artist? How can I humiliate her every time the "What does your daughter do?" question slaps her in the face? How do I reassure my family that although I am making next-to-nothing, yet working close to a hundred hours a week, that I can afford to treat them to dinner, much less take care of them in a few years (as expected of any Chinese daughter)? How do I explain to my grandparents, who don't speak English and grew up in 1930s China, that I co-founded a web magazine and am producing a documentary to explore the visibility of Asian Americans in pop culture since the inception of new media? How do I express my inescapable passion for the arts when my Chinese is as elementary as my mother's English and there exists an impossible disconnect in communication? Imagine not being able to have a single deep conversation with your mom…

Such is the constant struggle in the arts the general public often misconstrues. Even in reconnecting with a friend currently in med school, he described acting as, "just memorizing lines and lying to people, right?" This stigma, shocking as it may be to fellow actors, is understandably how those who have never experienced it perceive it.

Granted, I am merely learning to crawl, but in just my infant experience, I've fallen down enough times and had my emotional boundaries stretched to the point that I have an amplified appreciation of those who have mastered it. Yes, "memorizing lines" is step one, but it takes years to perfect the ability to deliver lines and portray emotions in a truthful and genuine enough manner to captivate an audience, to throw them into a story to the point that they lose track of reality, lose themselves, and empathize in tears and laughter.

What's more, there are dozens of other factors outside of acting one must focus on: once I had to let two dozen photos fall out of my dress, and all of them had to land perfectly facing up, spread apart, but only after one particular photo landed face up two feet in front of me. This took nearly thirty attempts, while I simultaneously reacted to the love of my life in surprise, bliss, then humiliation, when in fact I was looking at a blank wall.

But let's take a step back and appreciate the rare victory of even booking a project. Imagine going on a job interview three to ten times a week, every single week. Actors constantly audition, and constantly face rejection. The audition room can likely boast thirty-five girls who look just like you (or much better than you, depending on which side of the bed you woke up on). On your really lucky days [sarcasm alert], three hours of waiting later, you get three minutes with the casting director and a slim chance of getting a call back, much less booking the job. If you do, the shoot can be 7am-9pm, or better yet, 9pm-7am, and due to the primarily freelance nature of the career, you never know when and where your next paycheck will come from.

Take any other profession, and as challenging as it may be, there's a set path. Let's Google "how to become a..." Doctor: med school, residency, fellowship, doctor. Accountant: bachelor's degree, CPA exam, accountant. Actor: theater major or acting classes, move to Los Angeles or New York, send headshots to every agency and casting office, network, and persevere—a euphemism for *yeah, good luck*. Hard work and talent aside, you need equal parts passion and luck. For anyone to take you seriously, you need union, network television credits. But to get those credits, you need someone to take you seriously enough to give you that audition. It's a catch-22. Every successful actor has a different story, and every one of them had to find their own way to make it.

So why do it? Why even bother? Because life is fueled by passion. Whatever can give you that electrifying, intoxicating, unstoppable enthusiasm to wholly live, you owe it to the world to acknowledge it, pursue it, and most importantly, share it. There exists nothing else in my life as utterly and unconditionally pure as the arts. I belong with dance and acting. When mind, body, and spirit are perfectly in sync, and I let go of all fear of being vulnerable in front of others, to unabashedly share my soul—in that single moment—*I feel alive.* I find my perfect place in the world. Convention says you can't skip down the street if you are happy without looking crazy, or yell at your boss when you're angry at him because you'd get fired, but acting applauds the display of true emotions. Acting allows me to do what society tries to make us hide. Acting lets me connect with fellow human beings on a level far deeper than words. Everyone has a story to tell. My passion and mission in life is to help tell these stories through acting, dance, and film; to inspire and connect people via the arts.

In the last breath of daylight, I spot a driver eyeing the stupid smile that contemplatively appeared on my face. Embarrassed, I quickly revert to a more "appropriate" countenance… *No, screw that.* I turn on the radio and start belting out the lyrics. Hell, I'm even rolling down the window.

# Is Enough Ever Enough?

My boyfriend's father passed away. The phone is hung up now but it still rests in his palm as he sits there, broken, on his knees. This is the first he has heard from him in almost a year. All this time he has been waiting for news, any news from him, but this was sadly not the kind of news he wanted to hear.

His father, Carl, had been homeless for over twenty years battling his addiction with alcohol on the streets and in shelters. My boyfriend had flown him in as well as his best friend, at his father's request, to live with him and undoubtedly to try and save him. But it was asking a wolf to behave like a dog and, after more than a year, they parted ways a little sourly.

Regrets soon fill my boyfriend's head. He cannot stop thinking about all the things he could have done differently and all the things he should have said if he had but one more day with his father. There were some amazing moments, some happy memories, but those are not the ones that come back to haunt him. He is in a dark place. He blames himself.

But *how*, I wondered. In my mind he did everything humanly possible to help Carl. He welcomed him into his home, accommodated his homeless best friend and literally gave them the shirts off his back.

He offered them jobs, took them out to see the world and dealt with their substance abuse in the best way he knew how. He opened his heart, his mind and his life to these people he barely knew. What more could he have done? How could he feel responsible for his father's fall to pancreatic cancer or for a chronic depression that started long before he was born? Is enough ever enough?

I put myself in his shoes and thought back to my mom and our relationship. What if she was suddenly gone tomorrow? Would I overflow with wonderful memories or be gradually destroyed by my regrets? Even though my mom and I have a great relationship, she still drives me all kinds of nuts: small nuts, big nuts, chestnuts, walnuts, hazelnuts and even coconuts. It seems that no matter how much I love her and no matter how much she loves me, we cannot go through a certain length of time without driving one or the other crazy. It is hard to believe sometimes that, in spite of my most diligent efforts to be the most gracious daughter I can be, I cannot avoid running into hearty disagreements with my mom.

We fight about the usual conflicting mother-daughter viewpoints: personal boundaries, divergent priorities, missed expectations, plain misunderstandings, projected fears, et cetera. Interestingly, the toughest part is mediating her emotion-driven negotiation style versus my less sensitive, logic-driven reasoning. The problem then tends to become firmly entangled with each person's ego instead of remaining centered around the substance of the initial disputed point. This is when I feel guilty, wishing in silence I had turned the other cheek sooner. After all, I should know better.

Consequently what if this was my mom's last memory of me? In every instant, am I truly putting forth my most valiant effort to be the best daughter I can be? I know I did not in the past, but today I am different. I am forever changed, motivated by love and compassion. I simply want to be the best daughter I can be. I know I am far from perfect but I fear no failure.

In his passing, Carl gave me hope. He reminded me that I cannot alter the past, no matter how hard I try, but I can always modify my future and *that* is the beautiful thing about life. It is only by completely letting go of the past, moving on and focusing now on being the person I want to be today, that I will keep growing. Change does not happen tomorrow, it happens today or not at all.

Carl, I just hope one day your son will realize that while he may always feel there was more he could have done, as long as he did the best he could at the time, there is nothing he should regret.

"'Ohana means family – no one gets left behind, and no one is ever forgotten."

# Cuts Both Ways

It was a weekend of reawakening, of soul searching and of moving on. I call it a weekend of love woes. I allowed myself to be entangled in the drama, name calling, and blame hurling. I was in an emotional muck, answering its deafening banging on the door of my heart. I never thought I would get sick of the push and pull of emotional tides, but my heart finally caved in. I will always fight for love, conforming only to what my heart tells me. My head thinks too much, so it's simpler for me to follow the dictates of my heart. I only use my head when I reason that for as long as I don't hurt or step on anyone my decision will always be the right one, failing to realize that I am hurting someone—myself. I am waving my white flag; throwing in the towel. This time I surrender, realizing I can't position my heart on the path of 'settling' anymore.

I finally became weary of dwelling on my unending emotional issues just as my friends got tired of hearing the same story repeatedly. I now have gathered every ounce of strength left in me and accepted the reality that there are things that you have no control over. Even if you pray hard and do everything by the book, when fate has other plans it changes everything. It's heartbreaking. We've all been through love dilemmas, but do we ever really learn from it? When you're in a relationship, do you give it your best all the time?  Are you able to truly experience and embrace the whole romance when your head rules your heart?  But if you don't use your head, you suffer the consequences when it doesn't work out. So, it really cuts both ways, doesn't it?

I suppose it hurts either way too, just a difference in degree. Maybe it has something to do with change—be it a good or a bad one.  It is still a change.  You may lose something but you also gain another. I discovered that when you lose with grace and move on, you gain knowledge of your mistakes. You start to understand why things happened. Both parties have justified reasons. You start to empathize with the person who hurt you. You accept accountability for your part of the mess and then you pray again and hope for the best-unexpected thing to happen. This is what you gain the most—maturity.

In *One Hello*, Jazz and R&B singer Randy Crawford poignantly expresses that love starts with a simple "hello." After this hardest beginning, love may blossom or it may end. Falling in love is a risk. You'll never know if it will succeed or not. It's a definite gamble. People who've been in love and hurt and yet aren't afraid to risk again are the brave ones, the courageous ones. It is so because you give the other person the capability to hurt you – only people you love have that power.

I've learned to take it easy and just 'go with the flow.' When we accept and move on, it opens up new beginnings for us, and I don't mean move on by dating other people, but a journey towards inner change.  We can now courageously answer questions we purposely neglected before. You will be surprised what revelations you discover. We become true to what we feel. We become open to new possibilities, and thus the road to healing begins.

I am thankful for my family and friends, whose support has made this ordeal bearable. Anyone who has been in this position will agree with me that family and friends are truly a source of strength. Just to see their beautiful faces assures me that everything will be okay and that I am not and will never be alone. No matter what happens, they will always be there and make sure to catch me when I fall.

# Finally Found

For a 10th grade history project, we were divided into several groups and given an assignment to cover events that happened over the decades. "Be creative. Immerse yourself in the stories. Become the history!" the teacher said. My group had eagerly chosen to cover the 1970s. When I think of this era, I think of Woodstock and the hippies, social activists and their fight for world peace and of course disco and John Travolta in *Saturday Night Fever*. The first parts of planning and discussion were fun; we talked about dressing in bell-bottom jeans, acting as flower children and even making the boys wear platform shoes. Our teacher had to remind us that the '70s were also difficult times for America: Watergate, increases in unemployment and inflation rates, the Oil Crisis …

"…and don't forget the Fall of Saigon", the teacher said. Everyone looked at me, the lone Asian girl of the group, and they automatically chose me to talk about this piece of history in our project. It was assumed that being Asian, I would know this already. I thought to myself that this should be a piece of cake. I am Vietnamese after all; what wouldn't I know?

Moments later, it dawned on me that I didn't know very much at all. I felt embarrassed and ashamed of my lack of knowledge, not only of the war, but of my heritage and family history. I sat my mother down that very night as I figured she would be the perfect resource. As I asked her to tell me her story and explain how she got to America, it would become the pivotal moment where my perceptions of her, myself, my family and culture were changed forever. Since it was painful for her to talk about, she hesitated at first. She'd kept her silence over the years as she had no reason to talk about her past.

In 1980, far after the Fall of Saigon in 1975, the remnants of war still lingered. My mother escaped Vietnam, at the age of eighteen, with the help of my father who was fighting for the South against the Communists. He said that if she escaped with him, he will make sure that her mother and two sisters will make it to America safely. A heartbreaking decision made out of desperation and minimal hope, she was forced to take her chances. With a tiny boat that fit only a handful of people, they reached a small refugee camp in the middle of the night. My father was injured during combat as he was throwing a grenade that exploded too early from his right hand. My mother described the smell of blood and fear of his death would leave her with nothing. Over months, she nursed him back to health and they continued on with their journey. Quietly submerging themselves in black water, they climbed onto another boat, fitting about twenty people. This time the risk was far greater since they were covering larger bodies of water and the possibility of being pirated was common. They spent days and nights on this boat and as hunger was growing, hope was diminishing. In the day time, dolphins would often swim alongside their boat keeping them company. For a few moments, their presence would bring everyone peace, drawing their thoughts away from their worst fears. People would often joke with them, asking them to trade places and what they would give to swim freely.

One night they caught sight of a large ship and everyone swarmed with relief. People stood tall on the boat frantically waving their hands and screaming, "Over here! Save us!" Some unclothed themselves and lit their garments on fire, anything to get their attention. To their surprise the ship drifted further away ignoring their pleas to be rescued. Everyone was devastated, angry and confused. After a few hours, their boat continued to drift into nowhere and the crying finally came to a silence. All hope seemed lost.

My mother prayed a lot, just as her father did. He ran a Buddhist temple in Saigon and often spent most of his hours praying and helping the community. He was a role model as he taught his family and his friends to be unselfish and to always have faith. Distraught by war, he wouldn't allow the Communists to take his life so he took his own by burning down the temple as he stayed inside. Mother prayed through the hours of the night until she finally drifted off into sleep. She dreamt about him that night, and what a pleasant dream it was to see her father's face again, a face that she missed so much. In this dream, he kept telling her to wake up. "Child, there is something that you must wake up to see." My mother wearily opened her eyes to see dim lights ahead of her. She started yelling for everyone to wake up. With everyone's effort, they paddled quickly towards this structure in the middle of the ocean. They finally reached the oil rig and the crew, who pulled up each person to safety. They were finally found.

After months in a Thailand refugee camp, my mother and father finally entered America in 1983. I was born in 1984. Over a few short years, my grandmother and her younger sister made their way over to start the new life America had to offer, a free life. Her older sister never made it to the States. It was said that her boat was pirated and she has not been seen or found since. This still devastates my grandmother today, losing her husband and eldest daughter through war.

When my mother was done speaking, we found each other both in tears. We were crying because of the sadness of her story but then they quickly turned into tears of joy and gratefulness. My love and appreciation for her grew exponentially as I realized, for so long, she was working hard to provide me the life I have today. I have always been pretty comfortable and happy in my skin, even though I was teased and bullied in my younger years. I'm sure my mother wouldn't have it any other way as she brought up a confident and free-spirited daughter. My mother is skillful, independent, and most of all a survivor. Her story included loss and defeat but it did not damage her spirit or faith.

Life has not always treated everyone well or kind. We all bear scars, physical or emotional, but these scars are reminders of our triumphs and lessons we've learned in life. To learn the history of my mother's journey was to also discover a piece of my own identity. Filled with a new sense of Vietnamese American pride, I couldn't wait to share my piece of history with my class.

Steering away from hand written index cards with a list of facts and dates, I told the class my mother's story as a result of the fall of Saigon. Immersing myself in her story, I felt I lived it. I am a living result of it. I embrace the beauty of the Vietnamese culture and I am grateful for the birthright of freedom that America has given me.

I often think about her story as a reminder to keep me grounded and to appreciate simplicity. I am inspired to convert my energy into positive actions so her hard work and teachings weren't done in vain. Her story is one out of many and I encourage you to listen to someone else's, perhaps your parents'. Tell your story to someone for they can find something valuable in it too. My mother's story has taught me to live a peaceful and loving life. Ask your parents about their story. What will you find about yourself?

# Two Worlds, One Life

I stood in front of the bathroom mirror before heading out the door to my first day of school. I raised my head until my eyes met my image in the mirror. The face that looked back at me looked normal, like any other six year-old boy in the world. The only thing that stuck out about me was my size. I was small for my age.

"Kaoru, you don't want to be late for your first day of school," yelled Mom.

"Okay Mom, coming," I said.

Before my mother sent me into the classroom, she admonished me to be a good boy and to always listen to my teacher. I nodded, so she'd know that I understood her.

The teacher, a woman in her early sixties, began to take attendance. I waited patiently for my name to be read off. I heard names like "Adams, Jones, Miller, Roberts . . ." Then, she paused for a moment before saying, "Shin-man."

I quickly raised my hand and said, "Here!"

"Did I pronounce your name correctly, Kaoru?" asked the teacher.

"No, it's Shi-mon. The first 'n' is silent. It's Japanese."

"You don't look Japanese."

"I'm half Japanese and half white."

"Who is Japanese in your family?"

"My father."

"Was he born in Japan?"

"No, he was born in Hawaii, like me. My grandpa is from Okinawa. That's in Japan."

She listened, took it all in, and then continued to take attendance.

A short time later, the bell rang loud, blaring, for recess. It was a mad dash for the door.

"Children walk, don't run, we've got plenty of time," the teacher said, raising her voice.

But despite her order, the children raced around the school yard, laughing and pushing and shoving each other. The line for the spiral slide was filled with excited kids. Others swung on the monkey bars with delight. As for me, I was content to find an empty patch of dirt to play with my Matchbox cars.

Then, out of nowhere, a voice shouted at me. "Hey Jap!"

Startled, I jumped back. It was one of the boys from my class, along with a bunch of other boys I also recognized. They were all laughing at me.

"Look it, we scared the Jap," one said.

I sat there looking up at them, frightened, wondering why they were picking on me. I didn't do anything to them. I didn't even know any of them.

Then, they got in my face, pulling their eyes to mock my ethnicity. They imitated someone speaking Japanese. I started to cry, and when the tears began coming down my cheeks I ran away.

For years I was haunted by this memory. I remember waking up many nights with this intense nightmare because of this experience. I grew to hate who I was.

This was the first time that I experienced racism and being bullied. My life was forever changed at this point, and it affected the rest of my life, particularly my school years. I hated school, and never looked forward to it, as I had before.

I felt sure that it wouldn't be like this if only I were in Hawaii. Surely, people would accept me because I was born there. So when my father announced we were going to Hawaii for a vacation, I was so happy. Finally I would be in a place where I was not ostracized and bullied for being different.

The first thing a relative said to me was, "hapa haole boy." I thought it was a cool nickname or something, until I found out that it was a derogatory term that meant "half white foreigner." I was let down and disappointed to learn the real meaning. I was 2,900 miles from my old home, back in the land where I was born, and still, nothing was different. I wondered, "Will I ever fit in anywhere in this world?"

Flash forward ten years into the future: I'm sixteen years old, ready to get a job and this led to my next difficult dilemma regarding my ethnicity.

As I was filling out an application, I came across a section with check boxes. I was to identify my race/ethnicity origin. The question was incredibly difficult because it clearly instructed that I was allowed to check only one box. I sat there, pen in hand, wondering what I should do. After a long and careful deliberation, I decided to go ask the woman who gave me the application how I should answer this question.

"Choose the box that best describes your racial identity," she said.

Her answer didn't help me one bit. I wondered, "Will I ever fit in anywhere in this world?"

Flash forward twenty-three years to the future: I'm thirty-nine years old and married to a woman from Japan. She asked me if I knew the meaning of my family name. "No, no one ever told me what it meant," I said.

After she told me, I had a strong curiosity to know more about this name, so I asked my father about the family name, Shinmon.

My grandfather was eighteen years old, living in Okinawa. His family heard about an opportunity of a lifetime in Hawaii. Plantation owners were hiring people to work in the pineapple and sugar cane fields. His family told him that it was time for him to be a man and begin his own life. So began his journey into manhood. On the voyage to his new homeland, he wanted to do something memorable to mark this occasion, so he decided to change his family name. He spent day after day thinking about it until he came up with one that best represented this moment in his life. He chose the name "Shimon," "shin" meaning "new," and "mon" meaning "gate."

From that point on I held my head high, when I said my name. It was no longer a burden but a trophy that I held with pride. Now as I step through my life I envision each step as though I'm walking through a new gate.

Flash forward ten years to the future: I'm forty-nine years old and have just begun my journey to self-discovery. I've lost my job, I'm divorced, and I am living without hope. There seems to be nothing to live for, no dreams to pursue in my life.

Luckily, one phone call to a friend changed everything. She simply said, "You can continue having your pity-party or you can choose to push on." Her remark hit me like a ton of bricks. She allowed me to realize that my situation had nothing to do with anyone else. It had everything to do with me. I had spent a lifetime blaming others for my failures, because of how I had been treated by people throughout my life.

Things changed in that moment, and suddenly I was ready to take on a whole new attitude, and that's exactly what I did. I traded my old thoughts for new and improved ones.

I grew up in a time when people didn't recognize that labeling and bullying could have long lasting negative effects on a child. In my childhood, labels were placed on me by others because it was accepted as innocent fun. In other cases, the motivation to label me was simply mean-spirited, and nowadays we might consider it bullying. The pain and suffering I felt in those days is no longer present; it has been replaced by love, long ago.

It took me a lifetime to realize that I am unique. Of all of the people who have come and gone on the earth since the beginning of time, not one of them was exactly like me. It was divinity and existence that birthed me, and I know that I am here for a reason. I'm proud of my ethnicity, because it's a miraculous thing to be me. I know that nowhere in the world will there be another person like me.

SAHRA V. NGUYEN

*Translated from Vietnamese to English*

# A Letter to My Daughter

Dear Trang,

Don't you know your own mother anymore? You are my child but when you act like that it makes me feel like you've forgotten about me. You think you are so grown up now but you've barely begun to see the world and luckily, you will never have to see what I saw. You are only fourteen and slipping away faster than the hourglass of innocence, running away from me, from home and from who you are—my Vietnamese daughter.

The other night when you didn't come home or call, your father and I were slamming our heads against the wall trying to figure out where you were. Our hearts sunk in the midnight shadow, terrified of the unfathomable danger that could snatch you away in the city scowl. We even got into a fight about whose fault it was that you had become so disobedient. Don't you see how selfish you are acting? Your father's rumbling rage awoke the neighbors as he stormed out and drove around the city looking for you. Finally he found you on a basketball court hanging out with a bunch of hoodlums! You are an Honor Roll kid, why are you hanging out with those kinds of people?

I know you think they are your friends, but all guys want the same thing. You had better not get pregnant before you go to college! I'm not working twelve hour days washing people's dirty laundry just so you can hang out with some hooligans and get distracted down the wrong path.

I want you to become a doctor, then you can take care of me when I get old since we can't afford health insurance. If you don't like blood or needles, then you can become a pharmacist. Being a pharmacist is a great job—it pays well and you just need to give out people's medicine. There is even a CVS Pharmacy by our house where you can work at and be close to the family. What more can you ask for?

I don't understand you when you talk about following your dreams and becoming an artist or changing the world. Artists don't make a lot of money! Changing the world isn't going to pay your bills. Why do you waste your time with such nonsense? I don't want you to worry about having enough money to eat, making payments and taking care of your family in the future. That is the struggle of the poor and uneducated—you are better than that! Aren't your father and I already struggling enough for you? We break our backs day and night doing manual labor jobs so you will never have to. Look at my hands. They are so ugly from the heat and chemicals I toil through every day; calloused all over and aged with wrinkles twenty years faster than the rest of my body. I am so embarrassed by them. These do not look like lady hands; they are monster hands! You will have everything I never had, including soft, beautiful hands to play the piano and caress your children with.

When I escaped Vietnam after the war, you weren't born yet but I knew there was no future for my children there. The Communists had taken over, and I had to leave my village to go sell vegetables in the city. I was about your age. We were so poor; we only ate rice with salt, and sometimes if we were lucky we had potatoes. Trang, I know what it feels like to be hungry and I don't ever want you to suffer like that. Finally, I decided to escape with your uncle and it was terrifying. Anyone caught trying to leave Vietnam at that time would be persecuted. There were at least sixty people crammed into a creaky wooden boat; I thought surely we would die! Fear of drowning in the abyss, being raided by pirates or devoured by sea monsters consumed my mind and body; it felt like I was floating on the verge of death. I would close my eyes because staying conscious was unbearable; I didn't want to wake up but I wasn't ready to die either. Not everyone on my boat survived; some people fell ill and couldn't endure the tumultuous sway of the beast's belly, and one guy jumped in the ocean and drowned himself. Finally our boat reached safe waters and the hopes of a new beginning began.

Everything we have today, your father and I built from scratch. Can you imagine coming to a new country with no money, no family and no knowledge of the culture or language? We literally only had the clothes on our backs. It wasn't easy, but I've witnessed a war where people became prisoners in their own bodies; many burnt themselves to death in an effort to escape the hell on earth and be freed in heaven. After coming face to face with night demons and then surviving a dangerous escape across the ruthless Pacific, I knew there was no challenge we couldn't overcome here in America. Your father and I worked small jobs and saved every penny we made. Slowly we were able to rent an apartment and start a family. We leased a car, went on family road trips and bought a camera to document our memories. Life was beginning to look beautiful again. All of this was made possible with the money we earned through hard work.

Now you are beginning to go to those protests and get politically active. Why do you waste your time? It's not important for you to fight for these causes. Social justice is not a job! Don't you know there are Communist spies here in America? They will target you! Then you will make it difficult for us to go back to Vietnam to visit our relatives. You fight with your father and me, and now you want to criticize the U.S. government? Do you understand in Vietnam you would be put in jail for something like that? America has a great government. So much freedom and democracy! They helped us and many Vietnamese refugees come here after the war. I think you just like being rebellious. But you do not know everything. I didn't risk my life and escape a Communist government for you to stand out in the streets screaming for justice. I came here for you to have the opportunities I never had; go to school, make lots of money and be more successful than me.

I don't want you to think that I am money hungry or that I don't support your dreams. It's just—I don't know how to encourage you because I never had the chance to dream. Dreaming is a luxury. I didn't have the time or privilege to dream about what I would do with my life if fear and stress weren't constantly on my mind. I was focused on finding ways to stay alive—for me and for you. Yes, you have more options than me so please make the right choice. Our home, our food, our clothes—these things didn't just magically fall from the sky! Why do you make me feel like a greedy money hoarder? I just want the best for you. Making money gave me a second chance at life; and now you have the chance to go to school, make more money than me and have an even better life for your own children. Of course I want you to be happy; but even more, I don't want you to suffer like I did. I never knew what it felt like to chase a dream. I was too busy chasing a better life for us. They say money can't buy happiness, but money helped me rebuild a life and experience my greatest joy—being a mother. I want you to be happy, so if you can promise me you'll be smart about your choices, I will support you. I'll admit, you are teaching me what it means to dream. If dreams are about ultimate happiness, then the greatest gift these dollars have afforded me is seeing my only dream come true: you.

We have not sailed countless moons across the ocean and survived a generation of guerilla warfare because we are sugarcoated peanuts.

Remember that you will always be my Vietnamese daughter.

Love,
Mom

# East Versus West

I sat at the dining table, stabbing the bowl of rice with my spoon as my dad disapprovingly looked at me. "Finish up your food. Do you know how lucky you are to have food? People in Vietnam are starving." I crushed the fluffy rice until it was flat at the bottom of my bowl. I leveled the rice throughout the bowl, cutting my self-made rice pie into eight portions and slowly ate one slice at a time while I sulked.

He started the story again. Not the story of where he had to walk ten miles in the cold to get to school, but rather the story of how lucky I was not to suffer through the life my sister had as a child, drinking broth for sustenance because they were so poor. Besides being born premature, my sister suffered from malnutrition which made her weak and unable to walk until she was two. I, on the other hand, had a nutritious meal every day since I was born. This would not be the last time my parents would compare me to my sister.

While growing up, it was a battle of the East versus the West. I always felt that my sister had an advantage over me since my parents adored her by default because of her birthplace. She was automatically the golden child because she was born in Vietnam. She represented their past, and her presence served as a reminder of what they had to leave behind—their country, their family, the language, and the culture they dearly loved. Then there was me, the ungrateful, Western child. Every meal I ate, everything I had, my parents reminded me of what my sister lacked at my age. Guilt engulfed me, and soon that turned into jealousy. I was jealous that my parents loved my sister more.

The battle ensued, and it caused me to be resistant to the Asian culture in many ways. It was apparent when I lived on my own, away from my family. The Vietnamese language I was taught was left understood, but not spoken. Instead I responded in English. I attempted to retain my Asian heritage by decorating my kitchen counter with a rice cooker, but sadly it sat there gathering dust while as I succumbed to consuming pasta, salad and sandwiches. A bag of rice sat in my pantry for over a year before I even broke the seal.

My family tries to instill the Asian culture in my life, but I do not embrace it. "You are Asian," they tell me, but I beg to differ. I was born in America. I am an American. My ethnicity may define me as Asian, but I still am an American. I never cared to visit Vietnam, contrary to my mother's desire. She passed away, and never got that chance to step foot on Vietnam soil again since the night she escaped with my dad and my sister. Many years after my mom passed away, my dad sent me a poem that she wrote about Vietnam. According to my dad's translation, she wrote about her love for her home country. Even though they were oceans apart, in her heart, she would always remember Vietnam. After receiving a glimpse into my mother's heart through her words, I realized that my roots are planted in Vietnam as I grow and branch out here in the U.S.

Finally, I understood. It wasn't that my parents loved me any less than my sister. My sister was a link to their home country — a country they loved, but had lost. My sister was the reflection of my parents' past, my past, my heritage, my roots — the last link. They reminded me of what my sister went through, not because they cared less about me, but because they wanted to make me understand the hardship my family had faced. They wanted me to appreciate the sacrifice and the danger they'd gone through to give me a better life.

A daughter from the East and a daughter from the West. Two girls from two different countries bonded by blood. My sister is the representation of strength and perseverance of the past, and I am the light of hope for my family's chance to build a better future.

"Man's love is of man's life a thing apart, 'Tis woman's whole existence."

LORD BYRON

# Breaking the Cinderella Myth

When I was a child, my idea of love was shaped by my parents and environment. My parents were in an arranged marriage, set up by my maternal great-grandmother and -grandfather. Therefore, in my family, there was a strong sense of duty, devotion, and sacrifice associated with love.

My father was a traditional Chinese man from a traditional family, and my mother reflected the same customs, values, and morals. Both were confined by their cultural tradition, common in many ancient cultures, to marry for the purpose of starting a family, with less focus on romantic love. As new immigrants to the United States in the late 1970s, my father had to overcome many obstacles in order to provide for his family. Both of my parents sacrificed a lot to create a wonderful life for us and showed their love by working hard to make their American dream come true. My father was often busy at work as a doctor, on-call and moonlighting at night to support the family.

Because my father was so busy working and unavailable emotionally most of my childhood, I began to believe that I wasn't smart, pretty, or lovable enough to keep him around. Nobody explained to me that my dad loved me no matter what, despite his long hours at work, and that love can be shown in many different ways. But my negative misconceptions about myself grew and became deeply engrained within me.

What once was just a negative thought ended up becoming a negative belief system that started to influence other aspects of my life, mainly my opinion about myself. Eventually, it manifested into bulimia in my late teens and early twenties. It was only until I almost lost my life to this dangerous eating disorder did things really change about how I felt about myself. It was the ultimate wakeup call! I realized that the subconscious mind has the power to change the course of your life, for better or for worse, especially the thoughts and opinions that you feed about yourself. It's so important to treat yourself with kindness, compassion, and above all, love. You've got to love yourself.

Despite the practical foundation of love that I grew up with, I did not adopt my parent's traditional customs right away. In my youth, I was a bit of a rebel and veered away from my parent's traditions in search of my own truth and discovery of love, and what it means, both for self and others. Though I was influenced by my parents' model of love, I was even more affected by my environment and the Cinderella fairy tales that were fed to us as children about romantic, idealized love. I adopted a fairy tale fantasy about love and all that it could offer, seeking the Prince Charming who would fulfill all the wishes of my heart, feeding my innate need for approval, and complete me.

I attracted all the wrong men before I met my husband; men who didn't really want to be with me, men who wanted to use me, or men who did not hold the same ideals about partnership and marriage and were just along for the ride. My relationships with these men, though painful or challenging, provided a sound board for me to see myself more clearly, learn more about myself, and fine tune what I wanted and didn't want in future relationships. I discovered that Prince Charming didn't really exist, as no human being is capable of being perfect. But I also discovered that I deserved someone who could meet me halfway in a relationship, and someone who loved and treated me as graciously as I treated him. Rather than search for a Prince Charming that only fulfilled my needs superficially, I decided that in order to attract real love that will last, I had to be my own Prince Charming first. I had to heal myself and complete me. I had to give myself everything that I needed, make my life fulfilling, and learn to love myself, as well as being a good partner to someone else, before I could expect someone to be a good partner to me.

After all the heartache, highs and lows of love's tests and gifts in my twenties, I finally attracted my ultimate life partner at thirty. It was as if a light bulb had gone off in my head and everything just crystallized. I knew what I wanted to do with my life, and what I wanted in an ultimate life partner. Life and the pursuit of love had given me much to think about; I had wrangled with it, warred and negotiated with it, and experienced life and love in all of its glory. So at thirty, I surrendered to it. I realized that this pursuit of love was really a journey to discovering myself and of self-love. Gone were the days when I tried to fulfill a need to please and win approval from others. The most important thing was learning how to love myself, and make my life as fulfilling and amazing as possible so I could be a fantastic, equal partner to someone with whom I could build a life. It was the lesson of just being me, loving myself not in an arrogant or selfish way, but with the gentle simplicity of being truly content with who I am and my life and choices. It's like the adage by Elizabeth Barrett Browning but with a twist, "How do I love ME? Let me count the ways." Well, now I really know.

"Love looks not with the eyes
but with the mind."

WILLIAM SHAKESPEARE

# Breaking Through
# Real Love

Harry Kim, who was my puppy love crush in eighth grade, wrote in my yearbook, "Don't ever let anyone change who you are." Wow, wise words from a thirteen year-old that are still applicable today. He could not return my affections so found a way to share his sentiments in a kind and thoughtful manner. The journey of love is ultimately about acceptance and love of yourself. In a very simple way, his words served as a reminder throughout life to persist in becoming the person I was born to be, love myself for who I am, and be loved exactly as I am as well.

Besides loving yourself as a key to attracting real love, another thing women have to do is break, what I call, your Cinderella myths. An important reason why I think women are still single in their thirties and forties is because some women tend to live in a fantasy of what they imagine love could be, instead of facing the reality of what love really is. In my book, tentatively titled *Breaking the Cinderella Myth: How to Attract the Love of your Life,* these myths or fantasies that are engrained in society, in what Carl Jung's calls the collective unconscious, and our psyche prevent us from attracting real love or the love of our lives because we project a fantasy of what we think men should be and what we think love should look like, versus the reality of what is being presented and what it takes to make a relationship work. The truth is, in order to fully love another human being, with integrity and without co-dependency, you have to first know how to love yourself. It is not fair to expect another person to complete you or depend on him or her to fulfill your every whim and expectation and carry you through your relationship. Sorry, Jerry McGuire, but that is bollocks, and something you see only in the movies! I'd much prefer seeing women completely empowered to stand on their own two feet (or shall I say high heels), and take care of themselves financially, spiritually, emotionally, and psychologically. They must feel whole, passionate, and fantastic about themselves before letting a man into their life. That is one of the best ways to ensure success in a love relationship, when two people come together independent and grounded in who they are.

The truth is, no one can make you feel like a whole person, no one can really complete you, and no one can possibly rescue you and fulfill all of your fantasies. That's why they're just fantasies and not the real deal. Movies such as *Jerry Maguire, Titanic, Princess Bride, Pretty Woman, Sleepless in Seattle,* or *Dirty Dancing* perpetuate the unrealistic fantasies of idealized, romanticized love. You've heard the story before. Poor girl from the wrong side of the tracks meets millionaire heir or executive looking for a good time and some "lovin'," no-strings attached. They meet, fall in love, and then Mr. Millionaire runs around proving his love to her, rescuing her from her plight. Or vice versa, an upper- or middle-class woman in an unhappy relationship with a perfectly decent man who would give her everything in life, decides to break free from convention, and pursue the bad-boy, or man of her fantasies. These movie themes have been done time and time and again, reworked with the same plot and ending, with just different circumstances.

What I find completely absurd and unrealistic is that we've moved from fantasies about human beings to sci-fi fantasies about completely intangible entities like falling in love with angels and aliens. Remember the movie, *Starman,* in the eighties and *City of Angels* starring Meg Ryan and Nicolas Cage? In *City of Angels,* a guardian angel, Seth, played by Nicolas Cage, falls in love with a woman name Maggie, played by America's romantic comedy sweetheart, Meg Ryan, and falls from grace so he can become human and be nearer to her. She realizes he's an angel, but in her desire for earthly love, defies all logic and accepts him wholeheartedly. In a moment of ecstasy and happiness, while riding her bicycle, she closes her eyes for a second, extends her arms wide open, and gets hit by a car. Seth is then left alone to deal with the banality of human existence and enter the wheel of karma. When asked by a fellow angel if he knew the accident would happen, would he still decide to fall from heaven and be human, he answers with one of the most romantic lines in all movie history, "I would rather have had one breath of her hair, one kiss of her mouth, one touch of her hand, than eternity without it."

Now I'm not saying romance can't exist in a love relationship. I'm a sucker for romantic movies, comedy or drama, but I immerse myself into the films with the mindset that this is purely entertainment. These two-hour cinematic versions of love and relationships are just splices of life with all the challenges and boring, laborious details taken out. Living life is hard work, and love requires nurturing and maintenance like any living thing, but movies would lose our interest if they weren't short and sweet, with a nice arc, storyline and clear beginning, middle, and end. I'm not saying that you won't meet the love of your life that will fulfill your expectations. No one person can be your Cinderella or Prince Charming and fulfill all your expectations or carry an entire relationship. Breaking free to real love means allowing a person to be human, facing the reality of love, and loving yourself and accepting your partner just as they are.

These days, men are also looking for a woman who can meet them halfway, who can carry their own weight in a partnership spiritually, financially, and emotionally, be the mother of their children, and a true partner to them. Gone are the days when men were the main breadwinners in the family. Now, the recent economy in the last few years demands a two-income household in order to survive, and it's changing the way people view relationships and pick their partners.

I believe one of the reasons why the divorce rate is so high in the United States (54%) is because people too easily give up when things become difficult, they dwell in too much fantasy, or they are faced with a necessity to self-examine and resist it. Committed relationships and marriage force us to self-examine, and they give us an opportunity to grow and teach us about who we are, how we love, and how we should be loved as well. If we resist the need to self-examine, we live a life like a hamster on a wheel; unable to break a negative pattern or behavior, perpetually condemned to repeat negative behavior without the awareness to change.

Self-examination is the key to charting our lives the way we want it, and changing our destiny. We all have the power to change our lives at any moment and change it for the better. When it comes to love, it will still be hard work, but it's about having a positive perspective about things, and having faith in love. When you meet your ultimate match, the love of your life, you will have found someone who will meet you halfway and offer not 50%, but 100% effort into the relationship as well. A love relationship is a living, breathing thing that requires constant nurturing by both partners.

Just think about it. You hold each other's hearts in your hands. Therefore you must take care of this heart with the utmost thoughtfulness, and never take this privilege for granted. An ideal partnership is when two people are independent individuals with full, rich lives independently of each other, but when they come together, they are stronger together, champions to each other, and they challenge one another to grow. The truth is, all reality of life has moments of romance and fantasy, and love and long-term commitment can still happen for people if we just put things in perspective. One person cannot fulfill all of your needs, but if you realize that one person can fulfill most of them, and just re-evaluate your expectations, you can find love that will last a lifetime, and success will be yours. Living life to the fullest is about experiencing all ups and downs and details of life, even the tedious ones.

We are all fools in love! From birth to adulthood, love will test us, exhume us, entangle us, consume us, and enrapture us. The necessity to love and be loved is a universal and perpetual desire among all human beings on this planet. From the moment we exit our mother's womb, we are yearning for the feeling of being whole again, to be a part of something or someone. So our lesson in life is to learn how to love ourselves, and then to share that love with someone wholly, fully, and completely.

So how do you break the desperation of wanting to be loved or love another so you can wait for the real deal? Fill your life with a career you love, people who love and respect you, friends who aren't haters and genuinely want the best for you, and passions that fulfill your heart and soul and get you up in the morning. Fill your life with love and passion about who you are, who you're surrounded by, and what you do, and love will find you! You don't want to be the one of many; you want to be the one and *only* in someone's life. Realize you're someone special, and then go after your dreams and make your life special. Everyone deserves real, long-lasting love, so by facing the truth and realities of love, and loving yourself, you will achieve it. Let the reality of love be your happily ever after. Love is the greatest adventure in life!

Now go for it!

"Twenty years from now you will be more disappointed by the things you didn't do than by the ones you did. So throw off the bowlines, sail away from the safe harbor, catch the trade winds in your sails. Explore. Dream. Discover."

MARK TWAIN

# Closing the Gap?

*Nobody tells this to people who are beginners. I wish someone told me. All of us who do creative work, we get into it because we have good taste. But there is this gap. For the first couple years you make stuff, it's just not that good. It's trying to be good, it has potential, but it's not. But your taste, the thing that got you into the game, is still killer. And your taste is why your work disappoints you. A lot of people never get past this phase, they quit. Most people I know who do interesting, creative work went through years of this. We know our work doesn't have this special thing that we want it to have. We all go through this. And if you are just starting out or you are still in this phase, you gotta know it's normal and the most important thing you can do is do a lot of work. Put yourself on a deadline so that every week you will finish one story. It is only by going through a volume of work that you will close that gap. And your work will be as good as your ambitions. And I took longer to figure out how to do this than anyone I've ever met. It's going take awhile. It's normal to take awhile. You've just got to fight your way through.* – Ira Glass

I feel that what Ira Glass is saying does not just apply to creative and artistic endeavors, but to all areas of life really—people's professional jobs; their roles as fathers, mothers, sons, daughters, brothers, sisters; or, as students of any discipline, how they approach learning, how they approach getting better at something, how they evolve.

I also feel it applies to not just beginning artists, but to masters who continuously hone their craft. As an artist, I feel there is no "finish line" for skill, and one can continuously improve and get better at something – it's the journey, not the destination. As Bruce Lee said, "There are no limits. There are only plateaus, and you must not stay there, you must go beyond them." As soon as we decide to "stop learning" or say "enough," we should be asking ourselves whether or not we should still be pursuing this particular line of work. Because there is a certain joy and rapture in growing and developing your skills in any given craft, seeing your passions manifest after countless hours of fine-tuning and experimentation and disciplined self-study.

But this is hard work. Much harder than it sounds. It takes a certain type of relentless dedication, an almost obsessively reiterative process of placing oneself back on "a track" after falling off it so many times. But the drive is what is necessary and if we all know that if we really want to do something, there will always be a flame still burning – all that needs to be done is to keep feeding it, building it, and remembering that it is still there.

What if that flame is quelled, though? Fear is what extinguishes it. Fear stops us cold in our tracks. We are afraid of failure, rejection, alienation. However, in actuality we choose how we respond to fear, and so many times this response is already chosen for us when we don't even know it. Our excuses, so convenient and convincing ("I don't have the time," "I don't have the money," "I don't have the energy") are hard-wired into our unconscious. We are afraid to take the major risks to achieve great things – just because we have been hurt before. Soon, familiar voices populate our heads: "What if I fail?" "What if they hate it?" "What if they hate me?" "No, I can't do it. I just can't. Forget it." Our beliefs and our actions are already stacked against us, a default setting that prevents us from dreaming too big.

But learning to overcome that fear, and doing it over and over and over again, no matter how terrifying it seems, suddenly makes what we fear insubstantial. "I can't believe that was stopping me before," we say to ourselves. Confronting those fears, taking those huge risks and pursuing our dreams by going out there and simply "doing a lot of work" –having NO excuses – is the key to becoming a great artist and a great human being. The more we do something, the more we learn and improve, and the more we realize how fast the gap is shrinking between our ambitions and our own work. It's all just a matter of taking that first step. That first leap of faith. It's tough, frightening and intimidating as hell, but once you take it, you'll realize it was all worthwhile.

"Music gives a soul to the universe,
wings to the mind, flight to the
imagination, and life to everything."

P L A T O

# On Why I Love the Tabla

The bell-like timbre of the tabla is due to the soot eye at the center of the instrument. There's actually gum and iron filings melded in the black spot as well and to hear a thumb resonate against that occulus is to need to get up and pound your feet, throw your throat back in chant, or shake your groove thang. Surreptitiously I used to play these instruments when I went to temple with my family hearing the membrane resonate in my ear drums and blood stream, hidden from sight, not feeling like I was playing a conspicuous role as in front of the deities, feeling my forehead kiss the porcelain floor and breathing in the ghost and present feet of thousands of Indians. This might be Pittsburgh or Flushing, in the middle of steel mills or where a bustling Little India had sprung up, places where a community had sprang up.

Never at home but realizing I was a turtle inside out. Carrying my shell on the inside. Sitting on the frayed carpet in the wafting incense smoke, Lord Rama arrayed in a robe of butter, his bride Sita with a garland of jasmine flowers, and Hanuman, my favorite, the simian mover of mountains and symbol of strength and loyalty, at the feet of the two, looking up. Not at me. I looked at them, ornately carved from stone and intoned each day into divinity by Sanskrit slokas and dressed by curious priests with beards whose lives were spent smearing the deities with sandalwood paste and offering blessings to coconuts and bananas brought by middle-class Indian mothers. I was intrigued. Repelled.

These trips to the temple I grew to anticipate, especially because in the observance of culture I was immersed in myth, in the purity of a beam of longing, trying to hollow myself out like the drums I would play on the sly. I have been told by friends that I might very well be tone-deaf but have always felt a keen sense of the beat in my moving feet. But when one of my cousins would offer me his tabla set, the two drums, *dayan* and *bayan*, I would stall, my mind riffing on the real Roxanne, the Fat Boys, the origins of hip hop as I had come to encounter it in Northern Virginia, but that would not come out of my fingers in India sitting on the floor of a concrete building where the clothes hung from a line and a servant chopped vegetables for dinner. *Thwack* the beat sounded flat when I tried to raise it from the goatskin. Dead as a lead fitting. I grinned, demurred.

I think of the sound of the failed tabla now as a metaphor. Of what could have been but never was, an attempt at assimilation dead on arrival, a desire that far outdistanced the reality of wanting to find in a lack of musical aptitude at least some trace of connection, an ability to join the human jam with at least a pair of drums. I could have been a player! That's what I still to some degree think, never having taken lessons, never really played the tabla except in secret or momentarily as the drums sat on someone's cushions in the basement. The not doing has led to a perpetual could still do which permeates the day with possibility and makes clear that love surrounds us because there's always something left undone. And has left me with a love for the tabla, that Muslim invention, given rare form by Alla Rakha and his student Zakir Hussain, or the enchanting Suphala who plays all over Greenwich Village.

The elongated middle syllable of the table, the *plooonk* of a pebble in the cosmic lake, punctuated by the *dhadhin dhadhin tin tin ta ta* is what makes the tabla the living embodiment of primordial oneness, a familiar yet alien transmission, a language spoken by creatures whose synapses fire at a basso profundo lower than we can hear except as the rhythm which takes root in our hips and hearts. Dancing, never minding anything, but the music is love, the fullness of the moment realized, the water of the now carbonated to disperse. Similarly the slap of a thumb on the strung face of a drum is self-acceptance, which is a necessary prerequisite to empathy, without which any conversation about love is not worth starting. Even when the sound that enters the air burps like the final wheezing breath of a dying goat.

"The truth is that there is only one terminal dignity—love. And the story of love is not important—what is important is that one is capable of love. It is perhaps the only glimpse we are permitted of eternity."

HELEN HAYES

# Let the Shadows Keep Our Secrets

I want you to want me to meet the others you love. Though I'd be hard pressed to accept the invitations... hmm.

Is our game losing its fun as the real threat of being a passing whim grows or is it just that the desire to be more is impatient for recognition? Either way, I want the same things you do: My autonomy, Independence and fortitude. Like you, I want them to stand alone, unattached to others, without the infection of an audience and affected only by my individual intentions. Input from others is irrelevant as I know your worth and trust my instinct. I don't care to discuss my hearts, adventure with friends or parents... what will happen if/maybe/when... "let the shadows keep our secrets until then."

This is my head speaking from atop its loftier perch, looking down on my heart with a quizzical expression and mild concern.

My heart has an agenda of its own. A glutton of mirth and empathic of rejection feeling its crude path towards exaltation. Like a junkie, it beats a ragged rhythm banging the drum to rally my exception. Into oblivion.

Your spoken intention to preserve the peace and protect the broken heart in your near past is honorable. You do right by the one who gave you as much as possible. No fault can be found here and you deserve trust and patience... My heart says: "Beware the casualties of reluctance."

Down at my core the hum of physical satisfaction answers your call with eager reception and no walls. "Into me so we can consume you. Closer that we may expose our senses to yours. Deeper so you may swell within my ocean. More so that we may be each others devotion."

I can't warn you of the coming fractures especially since we heal well and faster. To ask forgiveness for the burdens you may never shoulder seems a selfish indulgence. These words circle but don't rest and may never come closer. Let's be honest, I won't go even if you won't say much. Until the need overwhelms you, can you stand by my heart and feel it gasping for air? ... From time to time, please slip me a sugar pill.

The real reason I write is to shed a small cast of light on my vulnerability. Even with this shield of esteem I am not unaware of my questioning... do I inspire shame, regret, or something worse? Nonsense!... Nonetheless, my throat tightens when I think like this.

We want space, freedom and more. We want adoration, this sensation, can't bear separation, with only modest hesitation... we hide our relation. It doesn't feel like denial but...

I want everything for you, though I may not always be the cure. I keep the hope that when you need to move will you have the strength to push as I must withstand the crush. Today I lack the will to let you go. Oh no, it's not really an option at all... I could try but I will fail. If a passing whim is what this is then pray you never tell a soul, for I will wish I'd kept tighter lips.

What am I saying? You're perfect!

# Dear...

Thank you for helping me move on and for inspiring my passions, I will never forget this adventure or the things you've contributed to my evolution. I save every memory, each moment we brought back to the world, the smell of your skin, and the beautiful sensation of loving you. I cherish you.

I respect your conviction, want you always winning, happy, successful, and with others who see what I see. Though I may not keep you, you should know that this has been the best I could have wished for. You're better than I imagined, what I want and more. You're magic to me and I see the horizon aglow with potential.

In the fertile light of your gaze, with the comfort of your strength, warmed by our persistent flame... I can breathe deeply and be free. I don't feel crazy but maybe too much imagination? Do you think I'm rash to offer these confessions?

What do you feel when you think of me? Do you see your life with me by your side or feel your strength rise when I'm on your mind? Are you comforted with thoughts of me and do you imagine the safety of my touch when things aren't going your way? Have you found joy in our union and do you feel me with you when you're alone? Do you seek my love and await my embrace? Will you miss me if I'm gone and hold on to the memories?

If you know me, if you trust me, then you know there is no safer place to save your love. You can put it on my shoulders, sink it in my stomach, drown me in it and we will thrive... all this and more, it will grow if you will give.

But I don't know where you are... Please don't make me guess. Where are you? Why do you hesitate? Why wait? You hate me. I wonder if you're aware of the price I pay. I do it by choice and almost happily, but am I an idiot? Do you understand that I'm the one paying this debt?

Help me.

I say to you, lay with you, sit by you, and sense the vacuum. If by the weight of my massive emotion or the lack of your contribution... the values are imploding.

Do you?

How much longer will I last? Have you thought of that? Do you care? My limbs stretch as I hold on, but the bone is pulling from my skin and though exposure is something I'm comfortable with, my naked soul is disturbed in this environment. I'm a shade of wishes drying in a desert. My steps leaving single impressions as I traverse this isolated path.

Ridges before me, lakes behind, the road is long and I tire.

There's not much to undo at this time. I'm not integrated into your surroundings and could disappear. An auxiliary indulgence you would miss for sure. You feel good in my care and when you want me, you want me there. More please, need it, miss it... my love, loving, lust.

I want your happiness and wait for you in silence. Here for you, there for you, in time and space, and wherever you go.

But...

Do you love me? Need to know. If you're unsure then you're a fool and if you're a fool then I'm the greater fool. By now you should have an answer.

If you don't love me please help me go.

# A Table Tale

On the morning of *Asanha Puja Day*, the townspeople bring offerings to the temple. By noon, the altar is brightened by the yellows and oranges of summer fruits stacked high against the stone robe of the Enlightened One. Monks scurry about the fragrant smoke of burning incense, ushering worshippers into the prayer room.

The woman hikes from her tattered hut at the bottom of the temple hill with a single, palm-sized bowl of sweet rice, which she had spent the entire evening before separating sticky rice grains from white rice grains to steam. She hopes that her labor can pledge her faith in place of the extravagant gifts she cannot afford.

When she reaches the doorstep of the pagoda, a few of the monks do not greet her and, instead, rush to welcome a town official. He has brought with him lavish, red-ribboned boxes of cakes and pastries, each carried by a different servant.

The woman is furious. She throws the sweet rice on the ground, stomps it into the pavement with her foot as she curses out the Sangha, and marches home. That night, she starts to cook again, rage in every knead of the dough she preps to wrap the meat of the housedog.

"Please eat," she says to the monks the next morning. The monks eat, but then vomit as soon as they are told by the woman that they *have just feasted on the flesh of an animal.*

*Years later, when she passes away in her old age, her soul is condemned to hell. For what she had done that day, she would have to sit hungry for eternity before a bowl of rice. When touched, it bursts into flames.*

"Now hurry up and finish your meal, child." Mom ladles bitter melon soup into my bowl, loosening the grains stuck to its insides. At my expression of distaste, she adds, "Drink all of it. It's good for you."

I fight the wincing and gulp it down. "And then what happens after that?" I ask her, the taste of bitter melon still fresh in my mouth. I eagerly await the happy ending to her story.

*The woman is survived by her son, a devout Buddhist monk. By the power of prayer and years of mastering meditation, he transports himself to his mother's side. He is heartbroken by the sight of her suffering and returns to Earth in search of a way to pardon her from her sins. United in prayer with thousands of other monks, he repents on behalf of his mother.*

Mom cores and quarters an apple from our garden tree, rewarding me with a piece as I push my empty bowl aside. "Only then is the woman pardoned," she says.

"And then they live together happily ever after?" I am curious.

"Not quite."

I squint hard at her.

"She is pardoned from her sins and no longer has to sit for eternity in punishment, but her life on Earth, as we know of it, is over. Story has it that she vows to mend her ways and do right by her son, perhaps, in a next life, but we do not know if they reunite."

"What was the point then if they can't be together? I don't understand." Some happy ending, I think.

"You will one day understand, child," Mom assures me. She wraps the leftovers and clears the table. "As parents, nothing we do is for the sole purpose of living together happily ever after. Everything we have done and everything we do now is for you later, whether or not we are still physically by your side. We do not need to feast on the fruits of our labor. Rather, knowing that you will practice what you learn from us is enough."

SONIA B. SYGACO

# Singing and Dancing
# in the Rain

I saw this morning's downpour, felt the sudden rush to go outside. The evening before, I'd counted sheep after sheep jumping over the fence. The *drip-drop-drip* from my rooftop had comforted my tired eyes, lulling them towards sleep.

Like a *camera obscura*, my eyes took snapshots of childhood friends walking homebound, caught unguarded from the crying sky. We pretended the steel bar paths were railroads, and immediately the field became an avenue for play: tug of war, catch and run, and tumbling on the grass, wrinkly fingers from the growing cold. We were unmindful if we had missed lunch. We didn't wear waterproof watches so we had to take off everything that would be spoiled by the wet, hiding all our bags beside the Luce lobby. Only when our lips quivered would we decide to head home.

I seldom had the chance to go rain dancing, in the passing of time. In fact, there had been many rainy seasons, countless to remember. Or perhaps one would refuse to remember them? A child would never forget. It's only when the moment becomes insignificant that another event unfolds to replace a memory. Looking through the child's eyes, one could see this carefree spirit, an attitude inherent from our past but beyond our reach. Was it because those little clothes would

199

no longer fit us now? Or during the transformation something did really change and so we became hunchbacks besotted with myriad responsibilities. Living outside the comfort zone, we depended on the weather. What options could one have, but to get along with it? One could see an intersection—a choice leading the other but it only ended up in the labyrinth, and we were compelled to glance at the wristwatch.

One raises an eyebrow, seeing someone presenting something mediocre or cramming to pull things together. Or forgetting those little desires and wishful thoughts of what tomorrow would be for us. It's simple to dream something complex: I could think of a window display artist, an advertising specialist or a war correspondent. Nonetheless, all the darts missed the red circles. The challenges continued, the rain smearing the glass windows.

Even now, I maintained the habit of letting rain fall my head, until someone beckoned me to squeeze in under an umbrella. Maybe I should be called an umbrella hiker. The rain shower constantly rolled my pants to knee length, as I waded and crossed the floods sweeping Manila. Sometimes, looking up became a crude way of knowing the sky's moods. Getting the warning ahead, all of us in the house would be reconciled to the ordeal of moving our things to the second floor. Waiting for the water to subside from the last step of the staircase, I set sail paper boats. It took hours, sometimes a day, to finally drain the flood gate. The merging wastes from everywhere: we had to buy mineral water to wash our bodies.

The rainy season was annoying, yet there were moments when I would rather accept the humiliating remarks, "Where's the rain?" But who cared? Well, they told me to break the rule of being an umbrella hiker. That I should bring one, gripping this rain gadget on a summer day. Else I'd have to endure multiple foot blisters from the scorching Penrith streets. I saw Aussie teenagers willing to tread on the hot roadbeds. The idea of being shoeless only happened in dreams, somewhat in fashion today. It was awful to see how they massaged lotion to soothe the cracked soles of their feet.

For most, summers are akin to favorable things. I should recount what summer is, how I admired the white-pink combination of the cherry blossoms near our old playground. For two months, that irritating and pungent smell would be gone, the trees turning bald, but for the bunch of flowers sprouting from the branches. I blurted: *summer fun*, where memoirs bridged the next getaway.

There is so much discussion about getaway or the passing of each season, which brings me to Sara Teasdale's *Spring Rain*. Love in the rain, for Teasdale, offers maturity and does not stay in a doll house, life being perfect. So the author recollects her love in moderation. It teaches her to handle disappointments from the storm that sweeps through them:

> *I remembered a darkened doorway*
> *Where we stood while the storm swept by,*
> *Thunder gripping the earth*
> *And lightning scrawled on the sky.*

When it rains, everything and all our expectations change. Planning life accordingly can turn awry. For instance, the intermittent fall of the rain during a pleasant day only confuses. For this rain that everyone tries to escape excuses no one. Others will immediately grab a mask so no one recognizes them or witnesses their fall. Or obediently they kneel when life dictates while others are too ashamed to admit. I am ambivalent; I will soon get ready for my Camden trip or wait in eternity for Godot.

Like me or anyone else, all of us are as destined as Prometheus Bound, whose fate is controlled by the cosmos: to toil for this year, next year and the next until the figures are alternating decimals, infinite as long as people exist. The rain will never stop falling, so generic and common. For such understanding of how the rain devastates is wisdom gained. I feel unworthy, glued and paralyzed as grief devours my emotions. I would experience death in every rainfall and resurrect to life when the sun comes out from its hiding.

Yet, people waltzing in the rain achieve more. It takes one to write a thesis in three months from the conventional one-year writing period, a single mother with four children, juggling between work and school, to become a lawyer, while another who washes his red shirt every night for tomorrow's wear turns out to be someone influential. My nanny's infant who was not breastfed but given coconut wine married a Swiss businessman. It is surprising, that this complex process gives birth to anguish then springs off—challenging the human spirit not to cross the river twice and instead aim for perfection.

So the rain drizzles in soft sprinkles and then falls in big drops. The bravery and courage of holding on makes it toilsome. There is a degree as to how far we hold off the threshold of pain—as thick as the rope or as thin as a thread. It is not possible to neither change the weather conditions nor alter the circumstances of the past. As Vivian Greene puts it, "Life's not about waiting for the storm to pass … It's about learning to dance in the rain." Keeping such a cheerful attitude affords a sense of focus and survival. And so whenever and wherever life takes me, I sing and dance. I sing and dance when there's rain or fleeting morning kisses from the sun. Singing and dancing in the rain, indeed!

# One Bowl of Pho
# Can Lead to Another

My husband is addicted to pho. It started innocently enough, when we met for lunch in San Francisco with Cousin Burt who took us to Irving Street, near 19th.

"I love pho," said Cousin Burt. We ordered our bowl, with everything, followed Burt's lead and sat there waiting for what we thought would be just a bowl of soup. It was, in fact, a life-changing event.

Our bowls arrived, steamy and fragrant with the heady scent of beef, star anise, roasted garlic and ginger. The bottom of the bowl was filled with rice noodles, tender chunks of boiled beef, a few morsels of tendon and tripe; the broth was clear and richly flavored, virtually fat-free in its clarity. Floating on the surface were a few shavings of onion and rosy slices of beef.

The waitress brought out a bowl of crisp raw bean sprouts, sprigs of fresh mint, Thai basil, cilantro, wedges of lime, and slices of chile. On the table were a cruet of fish sauce, soy sauce, a jar of hoisin, sirarcha chile sauce and a bowl of hot chile paste. We inhaled the aromatic steam that came up from the bowl, and began tearing this herb and that, releasing its fragrance then throwing it into the bowl, adding a handful of bean sprouts, squirting a bit of lime, dabbing in the hot chile.

One, two, three . . . Dip!

I plopped a bit of hoisin and some pickled chiles into a dipping saucer and every so often would dip in with my chopsticks a slice of rare beef, a pile of rice noodles. Then we took a breath to relax and sip tea. Then we began to add more herbs and more bean sprouts, so that no one bite was the same as the next.

It was like a happy frolic through the flavors of Vietnam and by the end of the bowl we felt invigorated though the bowl was so huge we barely got to the bottom – and we had ordered the smallest bowls. Afterward, we felt light, despite the amount of soup we had eaten. And by the next day we wanted to repeat the experience.

We woke up and after a bone-rattling cup of coffee, thought about eating our usual toast, and then Alan and I looked at each other. We didn't even need to say it: pho. We both felt the first stirrings of addiction.

ESTHER K. CHAE

# "Got Jeong?"

When I hear the word "love" in English, I tend to ponder the Korean concept of "jeong." Written 정 in Korean, 情 in Chinese. Pre-Google, I was always at a loss when I tried to express this word and concept to English speakers. Now post-Google, jeong is defined on Wiktionary.org:

정 *(jeong), pronounced as 'jeong' (sometimes spelled 'chung'), is a combination of compassion, empathy, and bond on a very soulful level. It is a connection that is formed between persons. Example pseudo-Korean phrases are: "That person's 정 is deep," "He has no 정," or "We live and die according to 정."*

Since language defines a person's thought and is a portal to understanding one's culture, if one's language does not have a word to express a concept in a particular culture, does the person therefore not feel these emotions?

My attempt of definition. Jeong = Love brewed with time + bond + endearment + warmth + empathy + a dash of pathos that brings a sensation of welling both in the eyes and heart. Most often unspoken and expressed through subtleties. Yes, it can also lean towards maudlin sentimentality.

OK. So. An example.

When I was a graduate student at Yale School of Drama, I would fly back once a year to Seoul to visit my parents, relatives and family. I would have to immediately make a round of formal house greetings to my hal-muh-nee (grandma) and elders. And yes, just like any and all grandmas of the world, feeding me was her way of showing me her jeong. I remember as a child looking up at my parents for help with pleading eyes and a belly ready to burst when hal-muh-nee would be annoyed that I was full and refusing her third helping.

Things did not change just because I was an adult, an acting student visiting from abroad. I remember that particular visit with hal-muh-nee, I wasn't staying long. I told her that I might not be able to come see her again before I left. She asked when I would be back in Korea. "Maybe in a year?"

She stopped eating her soup with rice in it. We sat silently for a while. She ate another spoonful of rice, stirred the remaining in the bowl and then pushed it in front of me. I ate the remaining and finished her bowl of soggy rice. I started to feel my eyes and heart welling. I understood that she wanted the same nourishment to be inside my body and become flesh and bone that would connect me and her. That was her way of infusing me with her great jeong.

She died the next year. I thought I was lucky that I was back for the winter holidays and was able to exchange a few words before her passing. My aunt said it was not luck but her determination that she would see everyone for the Lunar New Year and then leave us. Of course.

In my solo performance *So the Arrow Flies*, elderly Mrs. Park is the most beloved characters. She is a sixty-something, first-generation immigrant who survived the Korean War. A former linguistics professor who taught in Seoul, she now lives in the U.S. with her FBI-agent daughter. I believe one of the reasons audiences around the world adore her so much is that her character is infused with jeong.

## Scene 1
Mrs. Park/Living Room

> *Mrs. Park, 60 years old, FBI Agent Park's mother,*
> *Korean-accented and lively, enters.*

Hello! Hi! So sorry to keep you waiting, but my daughter Jiyoung just called and she cannot join us for dinner. She works very hard, even on weekends because she has a very important case about a North Korean spy. Oh, I didn't tell you? My daughter is an FBI agent! Federal Bureau Investigation agent!!! I like to say that, sounds very cool! Can you imagine, my daughter working for the American government.

My Ewha university alumni friends are scared of Jiyoung. But that day she was in a hurry, so she just came down the staircase without her jacket on and they saw the gun strapped around her. They said 'uh-muh-na, she carries around a gun?' So I said, ' she's FBI agent, what does she carry around—banana?' I don't know what they are more scared of. That Jiyoung carries around a gun or that she works mostly with white Americans, or that she is not married or because they think she is gay or because she has stupid horrible chestnut haircut! I think it's because of stupid short chestnut haircut. I keep telling her 'look at all those women on CSI shows, they have nice hair!' But she doesn't listen to me… But I understand. She's very pretty you know, so she can be very distracting to men. So she has to dull and mute herself, you know what I mean?

But most importantly, she has to be inconspicuous because she put some bad villains into jail. And sometimes the villains come back out to hunt the agent down. She has a photocopy in her desk of all the villains' faces who are now released from jail. She looks at it often to recognize them just in case they come after her. *[hushed]* So after I saw this on her desk- I secretly made photocopy of the photocopy. So I too can study very carefully each face-how high the nose is, what kind of skin color, what eye shape, how sharp their chin is.

I see everything. I have noon-chi. Noon-chi. Ah, too bad English doesn't have this word. It means "eye-sense". *[points at her eye]* Know what is going on. I have hyper eye sense. So if I see those villains from the photocopy, I can report to the police or call my daughter or distract them or do something, you know? So I can be undercover agent for my daughter! *[looks at laughing audience member]* You laugh now, but you are too young to understand. That is how a Umma's heart is, that is what I will do for my daughter.

*(Later in the play, Mrs. Park explains more about her daughter who the audience has only seen as an interrogating FBI agent.)*

## Scene 12
Mrs. Park/Living Room

My silly girl Jiyoung. She was always fighting when even when she was young. Tom boy, Tom boy. *[she shadow boxes]* Tough girl. But not because she is bully, but you know, it was hard for her growing up in a small town in Georgia, no Asians there.

I remember one afternoon, Jiyoung come back home, hit all over her face, dress torn, noise bleeding. I screamed "Jiyoung, what's wrong, what happened?" But Jiyoung just stared at me. She did not even cry, she just said she had to take care of some bad boys.

Then she went into the bathroom and grabbed the scissors. I was so scared she was going to hurt herself or someone, so I ran after her and tried to take it away from her, but she was already very tall and strong by then. And she look at me and said "Umma, don't worry. I'm just going to cut my hair." I said, "Don't do that, you have nice hair. Jiyoung, don't do that." But, she doesn't listen to me.

Then she just snip, snip, cut off her long beautiful hair. I just watched her. She stared at the mirror for a very long time. I think she forgot I was there because she jumped when I came behind her to style her hair to look better. And I said, "You are right, Umma was wrong. Buddha says hair is the weeds of ignorance. That's why monks are bald. You are too smart to be vain and carry around so much hair. I like this new hairstyle."

[*agreeing with an audience member*] Of course I was upset! My girl is so pretty and now she looks like Peter Pan boy. But I had to acknowledge Jiyoung's actions and kind of ritual, you know? Then I made a promise with her. "Umma will not dye or pluck my grey hair, so it reminds me of my old age and impermanence, and keeps me humble too, OK?" And then we made pinky promise. Sealed with a stamp. [*motions making a pinky promise*]

But that's all I could do. Make a promise. I felt very very sad that I could not protect my daughter more. And give her all that she needed and deserved, but I was so busy and tired working all the time. From professor to factory worker.

Anyway, so that's why I don't dye my hair. I know, I know I would look at least 15 years younger but I made that promise with Jiyoung.

Inspired by my parents and their parents and my friend's parents, Mrs. Park is an ode to all first generation immigrants and their concept of expressing filial jeong towards their children.

The Korean word 정's pronunciation jeong comes from the Chinese characters 情. It consists of 心(heart) + 青(blue). Not red for passion or pink for romance or purple for courage. But a **Blue Heart**. Talk about a bad ass-old school-one character tweet with so much poetic depth and meaning.

MARIAM B. LAM

# Northern Pho and Literature of the Global South

Every culture has its signature noodle soup, from American chicken noodle to cold summer Korean buckwheat, *naeng myeon*. Because these soups tend to evolve with the political and economic conditions of their respective homelands, each spoonful reveals an authentic taste of its culture's unique and complex history.

Peter Cuong Franklin of Adelaide, who researches the beef noodle soup, has attempted to trace the transformation of the dish from a regional specialty to an everyday national dish within the context of contemporary Viet Nam. He has found that the origins of the dish remain contested by different claimants, including Chinese "yoc pheu" (beef soup), French "pot-au-feu" and "an indigenous theory which ascribes pho as a relatively pure Vietnamese dish which came from Nam Dinh province, outside of Ha Noi." Franklin curiously seeks out possible antecedents of the soup and the beginnings of its use of beef. He asks, for example, is it possible that earlier forms of pho may have come from a beef eating Muslim Chinese group from Fujian that immigrated to what is now northern Viet Nam in the 15th and 16th centuries?

As with any cultural object of mythological proportions, its lore and stereotypes change with the seasons and political historical climates.

Some claim the Vietnamese beef noodle soup evolved from another Chinese beef noodle soup. Others argue Chinese colonialists made up those claims when they invaded Viet Nam for a thousand years. During times of relative China-Viet Nam peace, ethnic Chinese and Vietnamese sat side by side eating pho in Cho Lon, Sai Gon; neither could care less about the soup's true origins.

By 1979 when Viet Nam went into Cambodia without China's consent, they were no longer eating together, and postwar poverty-and-devastation-pho tasted of slightly salted water with a hint of precious monosodium glutamate and some occasional government-rationed rice. The Vietnamese would call this "pho that nghiep," or "unemployment pho." Those who made it across oceans and rough seas created new hush harbors they called *little saigons*, where they could proclaim with glee, "authentic pho lives again," and open pho shops on every street corner named with some lucky number. One named Pho Ha Noi served rare filet mignon sliced beef with a dark broth and no hint of irony.

In Australia, Cuong Pham curates an "I Love Pho" art exhibit with a catalogue of the same name published by Casula Powerhouse, while pho cookbooks such as *Secrets of the Red Lantern* crop up everywhere as colorful coffee table books. Art historian Boi Tran Huynh-Beattie documents such developments, while food historian Erica J. Peters publishes her essay, "Defusing Phở: Soup Stories and Ethnic Erasures, 1919-2009," in the journal *Contemporary French and Francophone Studies* 14:2 (2010). Some Vietnamese historians debate whether to approach the study of foreign presence and influence in Viet Nam as theorized forms of Vietnamese indigenization or localization practices, with pho as a possible case study. As academic scholarship on this novel object of study proliferate, the world continues to consume with little afterthought of its history.

Take Vietnamese literature as another case in point of divergent cultural trajectories into the global sphere. While the international literary establishment has championed Vietnamese writers following globally processed, English and French-translated novels by Duong Thu Huong or Nguyen Huy Thiep, and as the elite Ha Noi literary scene continues to promote a limited number of its own Northern writers, other northern Vietnamese authors, a Centraler such as Nguyen Ngoc, or a Southerner such as Nguyen Quoc Chanh, find very little circulation abroad. Consider if you will a fabulous diasporic Vietnamese poet, Phan Nhien Hao, who resides in Chicago, Illinois, writing primarily in Vietnamese with occasional English translation by his fellow compatriot, fiction writer Linh Dinh, who should have a much wider readership than he currently knows or enjoys.

As a body of literature globally surfacing after decades of war and centuries of colonial and imperial struggle, such penetrating, densely politicized and aesthetically innovative writing often gets passed up for "quintessential masterpieces" like the epic poem *The Tale of Kieu* or more accessible Vietnamese American writers in English as evidence that Vietnamese post-socialist literature has arrived on the arts and letters scene, a sanitized and potable scene following a familiar western war narrative.

So the trends continue—shrimp pho, vegetarian pho, tofu and lemongrass pho, Korean pho shops in Los Angeles Koreatown and Busan, Republic of Korea. This is regionalism at is best. Diversification can be good. Historically in Viet Nam, regionalized pho came with material constraints, classist jokes and stereotypes. *All* beef parts were said to have been used in the North. Fewer herbs and bean sprouts were available, masked by a heavier hand of star anise. Centralers were teased about a tendency to add spicy condiments until it was no longer recognizable as pho, a joke about the origins of *bun bo Hue*, or another special spicy red-brothed beef vermicelli noodle soup with its origins in the old royal capital of Hue.

In the South with its abundance of herbs, sprouts, lemon wedges, fresher produce, better quality beef due to international trade and mercantilism, there was little shortage of basil, cilantro, *rau ngo gai* (cilantro), chewy tendons or *xi quach* (tenderized meat cooked on the bone in broth), especially during the war years. The South also offers a delicious *pho ap chao*, or pan-fried crispy pho noodle dish, usually served with seafood, beef, chicken, pork and vegetables topped in gravy, an entrée that often comes in vegetarian option, as well.

Pho beef broth should be as clear as possible without any use of MSG, and this can only be accomplished with regular skimming of beef fats off the top of the pot as the broth simmers hour after hour. Today, however, you can find pho made-to-order or prêt-à-porter. Shrimp pho? You might as well have *bun rieu* (northern shrimp, crab, tofu and tomato-based noodle soup) or *hu tieu nam vang* (southern seafood soup with optional thick glass noodles). Vegetarian pho? Just have *chao* (congee), why don't you. These are all American and other bastardizations of original "gangsta pho." And yet, I along with many others, have come to enjoy the many fusion, hybrid and freak-of-nature oddities that the pho form has come to embody.

Individual tastes vary, as well, with purists who like to keep their hoisin and sriracha sauces separated in dipping bowls, while others like to fully saturate and dilute the beef broth with the sauces. Of course, with the pho regional stereotypes come gender stereotypes about Vietnamese women—intimidating Northern mothers-in-law, gentle and mild-mannered Central ladies, and firecracker in-your-face Southern broads. Snobby, elitist Northerners, hardworking rural Centralers, and lazy wealthy Southerners come to populate the stories we tell about pho in its national and global imaginaries.

As a cultural form, the world loves a good bowl of pho. It is only when a bowl of noodle soup, or a piece of literature, comes to stand in as proxy for some judgment value — against a people, a regional history, a cultured pastime, an intellectual capacity, a national worth — that its cultural value as a whole declines in the international global cultural community. In Andrew Lam's short story, "Ph(o)netics" in his collection *East Eats West: Writing in Two Hemispheres* (Heyday Books, 2010), he assembles a bricolage of chance global "*pho*nomena" sightings, from Nepalese hotels to Belgian castles. From Tanzania to Ubud, pho has truly gone global. But to really comprehend its language, its phonetics, one must come to appreciate its thick dark history.

If we are going to instead champion a newly "emergent" minoritized cultural commodity, like pho or *The Tale of Kieu*, then, let us admire it in all its mouthwateringly scandalous historical and geopolitical twists and turns. If we can see that deeply embedded and murky national politics through the clarity of a high quality translucent beef broth, if we can savor the subtle chewy texture of a fresh handmade pho rice noodle loop, if we can gnaw intently on the gristle left behind on a well-soaked beef marrow bone, if we can imbibe the complex aromatic flavor palate of its refined broth sup after loud and sloppy sup, only then will we have truly consumed a bowl of pho for life.

"We can let circumstances rule us, or we can take charge and rule our lives from within."

EARL NIGHTINGALE

# Kimmy Tang
## The Making of a Chef

Even if she wore a toque, which she doesn't, Chef Kimmy Tang's five feet three inches and ninety-eight pounds wouldn't give her the stature of a giant. But what's inside that deceptively dainty package is another story.

When she was born, on April 2, 1965, her skin was so fair that although her young mom and dad, ThikimThring and KienHoa, officially named her Kimdung, they lovingly called her "Mashed Potato." She was the baby of the family, sister KimYen and brothers KimLan and KimNhac having entered the world in 1960, 1962 and 1963.

Life was good for the young family. Their father, who started out as a teacher of economics and business management, had become a successful businessman. Propelled by a restless intellect he wrote books on Buddhism, created an English-Vietnamese dictionary, and translated Chinese history books. At heart he was a deeply spiritual person who took a personal interest in everyone around him, especially his students. It was an attitude they would remember in later years.

The Tangs lived in a spacious house in the ChoLon area of Saigon and employed a chef and two nannies to help Thikim Thring run her busy household. She was careful not spoil her children, teaching them to be respectful to everyone, including the servants. When they wanted to cook for Kimdung, her mom would stop them. "Let her do it herself," she'd say. "You never know when it will come in handy."

Fast forward to New Year's Eve 1968. Kimdung remembers: The Tet (holiday) table is laden with food. Without it we would starve. A watermelon drops and my dad picks it up and carefully cleans it and gives it to us. We gobble the banh tiet (salty pork and beans wrapped in sticky rice and banana leaf) and sugar-coated lotus. It tastes better than anything we've ever eaten.

Suddenly — Bam! Bam! Bam! What is this sound? Firecrackers? Who plays with firecrackers at midnight??? Oh, no! That is the sound of bombs! "Wake up! Wake up! Run to the living room," my mom shouts. My nanny, Chi Het, picks me up and runs with me. Bam! Bam! Bam! A bullet whizzes by just above my head and hits Chi Het. I start sobbing and sobbing. Like a broken blister her blood splatters all over me. My Mom sees that I am covered with blood and she panics. I am not even three years old, I don't know why Chi Het's blood is on my head. My mom cries, "Het, Het, are you okay? What happened? Don't scare me!" But there is no answer. Mom reaches out to her but as soon as she touches her, she realizes that Chi Het is dead. "Oh! Het, Het ...." Mom starts to weep.

Helicopters whir above our house: "Hello! Hello! Leave your house, we are going to bomb here," the military announce on their microphones. Dad says, "I'll get the car. Stay here. Don't move." His car keys are at the reception, which is about three houses away from our house. Dad crawls to the lobby. "Oops! Which key? God! Please help me find my key," Dad prays. Yes! He finds it.

"Let's get in the car quickly...Kimyen, pick up your sister. Alan, Simon please run fast to the car. Don't be scared, Papa is here. Sit down! Don't sit on the seat, sit on the mat. Please hurry up! We need to get out of here soon. Kim, Kim, let's go." Mom tries to pick up her dogs, Lucky and Happy, but they don't want to leave. Papa says, "Hurry up! We must go." Finally, Mom has to give up and jump into the car.

Ah! The gate is locked? Oh! What should we do? Wait, the gate is closed but the lock is not locked. (Sigh). The drive from Tan Xuong

Nhat Airport to Saigon is not far, but we feel like we will never reach our destination. Finally, Ding-dong! "Open the door, please…. this is Kien Hoa's family." My Auntie, who stands behind the door, asks, "Are you human or spirits [ghosts]? The Commander said your house was completely destroyed and none of you are alive." Mom says, "Yes, we are still alive. If you don't believe it, touch our chins."

A week later, the war is over and mom and dad go back to our house. "Lucky! Happy! Lucky! Happy! Where are you? Are you okay?" mom calls out. The poor dogs are sitting on either side of Chi Het's body. They are exhausted, starving and dehydrated. "Please, take good care of them please, please," mom cries to the fire fighter. Dad stares at the ashes all around him.

Soon after, they moved from the Tan Son Nhuc Airport district to the Cholon City Chinatown in Saigon. Kien Hoa worked as the CEO of a cookie and instant noodles factory, which mainly provided food for the American military. His interest in food runs in the family. "I remember wanting to be a psychologist when I was young," says Kimdung, "but mom said I was born to be a chef. She said I always played cooking games and, when we went to the toy store, the first thing I picked out was kitchenware." By the time she was five years old, she was helping in the kitchen and by the time she turned nine she was cooking on her own. After school Kimdung would set up a little kitchen and ask the family cook to supply her with real food, which she sold to the neighbor children. Her first business venture might have been a financial success except that she allowed her customers to pay with toy money.

This idyllic life ended after the fall of Saigon in 1975, when the communists swept down from the north, threw Kien Hoa in jail, and appropriated the family's property and material goods. When he was released, like many others the Tangs tried to flee but freedom was ten years away. Finally, after a seven-month detour in a Filipino refugee camp, with the help of an uncle who had already made it to the States, they landed in dusty Bakersfield, California. It looked like heaven. She worked in a Chinese restaurant while attending night class to learn English, a new language for her new life.

Kimdung Tang is now US citizen Kimmy Tang. She moves to Los Angeles, where she lands a job in a Japanese restaurant and enrolls at the Fashion Institute of Design and Merchandising (FIDM). After graduation she combines her culinary and cooking passions by designing and opening Michelia Asian Bistro on a shoestring. Inspired by old Chinese and Vietnamese recipes, she adapts French cooking techniques to southern California tastes, which beguiles critics from the *L.A. Times* and *Los Angeles Magazine*, and earns her a 25 food rating in the Zagat Survey. Jackie Chan, Collin Farrell and Larry King are among her adoring customers but she's a one-woman show and, when she gets an offer to sell, she takes off for Romania. From there she explores Europe and Asia, surprising her mother wih a reunion trip back to Vietnam which, despite its remarkable progress since the war ended in 1975, is still among the world's poorest countries.

While acting as culinary consultant for Romania's largest film studio, she appears on camera and hosts a TV cooking show. She also assists at a local orphanage and when she returns to the states three years later, she gets involved with children's charities such as the Blue Heron Foundation, Casa Pacifica, Children Hospital and the Special Olympics.

Today Alan (KimLan) runs a food factory in El Monte for Trader Joe's; Simon (Kim Nhac) is a copy machine tech in Irvine and Kimyen is married and living in San Francisco. Kimmy's mother divides her time among her children and though her beloved father passed away a few years ago, the greatness of spirit that he instilled in his children lives on. It's there in the charitable venture Kimmy is planning to honor him, it's in her unsung charitable deeds and, above all, it's in every bite of market-fresh Vietnamese fare she turns out at her three locations (so far) of 9021Pho — Beverly Hills, Culver City and Westlake Village. Of course pho is on the menu (*pho bo*/beef; *pho ga*/chicken; *pho ca*/tuna; *pho chay*/tofu), as is her legendary Michaelia Crunchy Roll; grilled beef wrapped in vine leaves; *mei-nam* noodles; charcoal pork salad; *banh mi*; and the panko-fried sole filet she tops with homemade French spicy *aioli*, one of her sauce creations that are so mouth-watering she's been asked to bottle them.

Who says you can't buy love?

# Recipes for Pho

# "A Bowl of Pho"
Serves 6 to 8

## Pho Particulars

In Vietnam, pho is mostly a restaurant food. Though some people prepare it at home, most prefer going to noisy soup shops. Here are a few tips:

- Pho comes with a variety of toppings including rare beef, well-done beef and slices of brisket, tendon, tripe and even meatballs. If you're a novice, try *pho tai chin*, which includes the rare and well-done beef combination.

- When the bowl arrives, eat it while it's piping hot. If you wait for it to cool, the noodles will expand and get soggy.

- Sprinkle some black pepper, then add bean sprouts, fresh chiles and a little squeeze of lime to your bowl. Using your fingers, pluck the Asian basil leaves from their sprigs and, if they're available, shred the saw-leaf herbs and add to the soup. Add little by little, eating as you go. If you put the greens in all at once, the broth will cool too fast and the herbs will overcook and lose their bright flavors. Chile sauce and hoisin sauce are also traditional condiments but I avoid them because, to my taste, they mask the flavor of pho. You, however, may like them.

- With spoon in one hand and chopsticks in the other, pull the noodles out of the broth and eat, alternatively slurping on the broth. It's totally acceptable and normal to be seen with clumps of noodles dangling from your mouth, eyes squinting from the steam and glasses all fogged up.

The broth is served in large amounts to keep the noodles warm and to help season the dish. It's not necessarily meant to be totally consumed. But if you do happen to be in the mood, it is perfectly OK to tip the bowl and scoop out every single drop.

# Vietnamese Beef Noodle Soup (*Pho Bo*)

You can prepare the beef broth in advance and assemble just before serving.

## Ingredients

**BROTH**

- 5 pounds beef marrow bones
- A 3-pound chuck roast
- 2 (4-inch wide) pieces fresh ginger, unpeeled
- 1 large yellow onion, peeled
- ⅓ cup Asian fish sauce
- 5 tablespoons sugar
- 8 whole star anise
- 3 whole cloves
- 1 tablespoon salt, or to taste

**NOODLES & ASSEMBLY**

- ½ pound beef sirloin steak, slightly frozen, then sliced paper thin
- 1½ pounds fresh or dried flat rice stick noodles (about ⅛" wide)
- 1 yellow onion, sliced paper thin
- 4 green onions, chopped
- ½ cup chopped cilantro
- 1 pound bean sprouts
- 20 sprigs Asian basil
- 20 leaves saw-leaf herb (optional)
- 3 tablespoons chopped fresh Thai bird chiles, or thinly sliced serrano chiles
- 2 limes, cut into thin wedges
- Pepper to taste

# Instructions

## BROTH

Bring 6 quarts water to a boil in a large stockpot.

Place the bones and chuck roast in a separate pot with water to cover; bring to a boil and boil vigorously for 5 minutes. Using tongs, remove the bones and meat and add to the first pot of boiling water. When the water returns to a boil, reduce to a simmer.

Using metal tongs, hold the ginger and onion over a gas burner until slightly blackened and aromatic. (If you have an electric stove, dry-roast the ginger and onion in a skillet.) Rinse the ginger and onion and add them to the pot with the meat and bones.

Add the fish sauce and sugar to the pot. Simmer, skimming off the foam, until the meat is tender, about 1 ½ hours. Remove the chuck roast and submerge in a bowl of cold water for 15 minutes. This prevents the meat from darkening and drying out. Place the star anise and cloves in a dampened spice bag and add to the broth. Add 2 cups water to the pot. Simmer for 1 hour, then remove and discard the spice bag and onion. (Cooking the spices too long makes the broth dark and pungent.) Add the salt to the broth and keep at a low simmer while preparing the noodles. The broth should be rich enough to serve after 2 ½ hours total cooking time. It will taste salty, but will balance once the noodles and accompaniments are added.

## NOODLES & ASSEMBLY

Cut half of the roast into thin slices; reserve the remaining roast for another use. Cut the partially frozen sirloin into thin slices. Place the sliced chuck and sirloin on separate plates and set aside. Bring a large pot of water to a boil. Place a handful of fresh noodles (enough for 1 serving) in a sieve and lower into the boiling water. Using a fork or chopsticks, stir for 15 seconds, then lift and shake off excess water. (If using dried noodles, soak them in warm water for 20 minutes. Cook them all at once until al dente, about 2 to 3 minutes. Rinse extremely well in warm water.) Divide the noodles among heated serving bowls. Arrange a few slices of roast and sirloin on the noodles in each bowl.

Bring the beef broth to a rolling boil. Season with salt (if necessary) and pepper. Ladle 2 to 3 cups into each bowl. Sprinkle each serving with 1 tablespoon sliced yellow onion, 1 tablespoon green onions, 1 tablespoon cilantro and pepper to taste. Let diners garnish their bowls with bean sprouts, Asian basil, saw- leaf herb, chiles and squeeze of lime as desired.

PER SERVING
90 calories, 28g protein, 51g carbohydrate, 6g fat (2 g saturated), 66mg cholesterol, 1592mg sodium, 2g fiber

# "What I Did for Pho"

### Serves 1 to 2

## Ingredients

- Vietnamese or Thai rice noodles (often labeled as "rice stick")
- 1 large beef shank (preferably from a grass-fed cow who's been treated in a humane way)
- 1 large stick of lemongrass
- ½ onion or three shallots
- Clove of garlic
- A good chunk of ginger or galangal
- 1 lime
- Salt
- Fish sauce
- Thai basil (optional)
- Cilantro (optional)
- Mint (optional)
- Bean sprouts (optional)
- Hoisin sauce (optional)
- Chili sauce (optional)

## Instructions

Put the beef shank in a large bowl of cold water. Let it soak for about one to two hours. This gets some of the impurities out.

Transfer the shank into a large pot and fill with fresh cold water. The water should completely cover the shank by at least an inch. Bring the water to a boil. As soon as the water boils, turn it down to a good simmer. In about five minutes scum should start floating to the top. Remove as much as you can with a skimmer or a spoon. To the cooking liquid add lemongrass (if using), garlic, onion (or shallots), and ginger. Turn the heat down to a slow, gentle simmer and cook the broth for some four hours. Keep checking every half hour or so to make sure there's still a nice level of water in the pot. If you need to, add more water.

After four hours, the meat should be falling off the bone. Which is what you want. Take the shank out of the broth and let it cool until you can touch it without burning yourself. At this point, remove everything else, like the lemongrass, and discard. When the beef has cooled, remove the bone and slice the beef into thin pieces.

Meanwhile, season the broth with salt. How much salt you'll need will depend on how much broth you have. Start with a small amount. Taste. Add more if needed. You don't want it to be too salty because you'll be adding fish sauce next, about a teaspoon. Keep tasting and adjusting the salt and fish sauce until the broth is the way you like it.

Now for the noodles. Rice noodles can come fully dried or partially dried. The fully dried ones need to be soaked in water for about half an hour and then put into boiling water for about five minutes. Cooking times for noodles vary greatly. What I do is check the noodles every few minutes to see if they're done, usually by dipping a noodle in cold water and eating it. The partially dried noodles need no soaking time. A gentle dip in boiling water should do the trick. But again, you must test the noodles as frequently as possible or you will get a mush.

To assemble, put the noodles in a warmed bowl. Garnish with beef and any combination of bean sprouts, cilantro, Thai basil, mint, etc. Slice the lime and squeeze lime juice into the bowl. Add piping hot broth. Flavor with hoisin sauce or chili sauce or both. That's the beauty of pho—you decide how it should taste.

# "What I Won't Do Pho Love"

Serves 6

## Ingredients

**BROTH**

- 2½ pounds beef chuck roast
- 6 cups water + 3 cups water
- 1 beef bouillon cube
- 1 tablespoon salt
- 1 tablespoon fish sauce
- 1 tablespoon sugar
- 5 whole star anise
- 1-inch ginger root (sliced into 8 pieces)
- 1½ pounds pho noodles

**TOPPINGS**

- Bean sprouts
- Thinly sliced onion
- Thinly sliced green onions
- Fresh cilantro, chopped
- Basil leaves
- Limes, quartered
- Extra fish sauce, hot pepper sauce (Sriracha), hoisin sauce (optional)

## Instructions

Put pho noodles in large bowl or pot. Cover with water. Set aside.

**BROTH**

1. Bring 6 cups water to boil in a large pot.
2. Put the beef in the boiling water. When water comes to a boil again, lower the heat to medium. Skim off the foam that rises to the surface and discard.
3. Add star anise and ginger to the pot.
4. Allow beef, star anise, and ginger to boil gently for 30 minutes, then add beef bouillon cube, salt, fish sauce, and sugar. Soft-boil for 30 more minutes.
5. Take out the beef. When cool enough to handle, slice the meat to bite-size pieces.
6. Add 3 more cups of water to the broth. Stir.
7. Taste the broth and add more salt and/or fish sauce as needed. Keep the broth at a simmer until ready to serve. Just before serving, return the broth to a full boil.

**NOODLES**

1. Bring a large pot of water (about 10 cups) to a hard boil.
2. Drain the soaking pho noodles and add to pot.
3. Stir the noodles and cook about 1 minute (or until water has come to a boil again).
4. Do not overcook the noodles.
5. Drain the noodles.

Place desired amount of noodles into each bowl. Top with sliced meat and sliced onion. Ladle the boiling broth over the noodles and meat. Serve immediately, and let guests add the toppings they like.

# "One Bowl of Pho Can Lead to Another"

Serves 4

## Vietnam In A Bowl

Pho is sometimes described as Vietnam in a bowl. All of these flavors and textures are there, from the North to the South: the rich, the hot, the pungent, the sour, the crisp, the fragrant, the tender, and the soft. It is a layering that trails the history of the land, from the Chinese-influenced beef-noodle soup that originated in Hanoi, through the spices of neighboring and conquering countries, ending with the freshness of toppings that is said to have been introduced by the French. No other country serves such an invigorating herb and salad plate, especially with a bowl of soup.

When you eat pho, the noodles slap around your lips, scattering droplets of broth over your face. And, if you eat like me, you may splash some on your dining companion's face too. Eating pho together is a bonding experience.

Back in London we found two pho restaurants: one was close by on Wardour Street so I met up with fellow food writers John Whiting and Josephine Bacon, then ordered up the big, big bowl. We were served a tidy small bowl. There was such a small amount of hot broth that my glasses did not steam up, not even once. Oh, it was delicious soup with a crunchy little salad of herbs, but we felt no frisson of pho-nirvana. Shortly afterward in Paris, we interspersed our traditional French meals of salads, meats, buttery creamy indulgence with bowls of pho. It seemed quite a good dietary move, healthwise, too.

Eating our merry way through the phos of Paris brought us from arrondisement to arrondisement, from dainty little Frenchified phos, with their subtle flavors and ingredients that had been put together in the kitchen, to the multiethnic Belleville, where we sat down to a big splashy bowl of strong and satisfying noodles.

Our passion — some might call it obsession — with pho is leading me to one conclusion. Next stop: Vietnam.

---

When I want a bowl of pho at home but don't have hours to spend in the kitchen, I made the following quick version by simmering canned beef broth with the requisite spices and aromatics, ladle it over rice noodles and serve with its classic fresh salad, herby and spicy condiments. While you won't get the long-simmered fragrant soup pho houses offer, this has the distinctive flavor of pho and the convenience of being very quick.

As a variation, chicken soup can be made pho-style: by using chicken broth instead of beef and substituting shreds of cooked chicken for the raw beef garnish; similarly, I sometimes use vegetable broth with diced tofu in place of the beef.

## Ingredients

### SPICED BEEF BROTH

- 1 (2-inch) piece of ginger, unpeeled
- 1 or 2 shallots, unpeeled and cut into halves
- ½ carrot, thinly sliced
- Pinch of sugar
- 4 cups low-sodium beef broth
- 2 cups water or chicken broth
- 2 or 3 star anise
- 3 whole cloves
- 1 cardamom pod
- 1 cinnamon stick, about 2 inches long
- Sea salt to taste
- Freshly grounded black pepper to taste
- Fish sauce to taste
- 12 ounces rice stick noodles
- ⅓ pound beef sirloin, slightly frozen (for easier slicing)
- ⅓ cup chopped cilantro
- ½ yellow onion, sliced paper thin and/or 2 green onions, cut into thin rings

### HERBS & SPROUTS

- 2 cups fresh bean sprouts, washed and drained
- 10 to 15 big sprigs of Asian basil

- Handful of fresh mint sprigs
- 12 saw-leaf Vietnamese herbs (optional)
- 6 Thai chiles or 1 serrano chile, cut into thin rings
- 1 to 2 limes, cut into wedges
- Freshly ground black pepper

**CONDIMENTS**
- Sriracha hot sauce
- Asian fish sauce
- Hot chile paste
- Hoisin sauce

## Instructions

1. Finely grate about 1 teaspoon of the ginger (don't worry about peeling); set aside.
2. Place the remaining whole piece of ginger along with the shallots and carrot in an ungreased nonstick pan and char lightly and evenly over high heat.
3. Transfer to a large saucepan and add a pinch of sugar, along with the beef broth and water.
4. Dry-toast the star anise, cloves, cardamom and cinnamon stick in a small ungreased skillet over high heat for a few moments.
5. Add to the broth and vegetables.
6. Bring to a boil, then reduce heat to low and simmer for about 30 minutes.
7. Season with salt, pepper and fish sauce; Remove the spices and vegetables using a slotted spoon.
8. Keep the broth at a low simmer.
9. Cook the noodles by boiling according to the package instructions; drain and set aside.
10. Slice the partially frozen beef thinly against the grain.

Into each serving bowl place a large portion of noodles (these may be cool and they may stick together – not to worry, they'll unstuck in the hot broth.)

Top each bowl of noodles with a dab of the reserved grated ginger, a sprinkling of cilantro, a few onion rings and 4 to 6 thin slices of beef.

Ladle the hot broth into the bowls and serve accompanied by the plate of herbs and condiments.

PER SERVING (ESTIMATED)

420 calories, 16g protein, 79g carbohydrates, 3g fat (1g saturated), 17mg cholesterol, 250mg Sodium, 3g fiber

# "Kimmy Tang: The Making of a Chef"

Makes 8 satisfying (American-sized) bowls

## Ingredients

**BROTH**

- 5-6 pounds beef soup bones (marrow and knuckle bones)
- 1 pound piece of beef chuck,
- 1 pound daikon (white radish)
- 1 pound shallot
- 4 ounce ginger (char and cut into 1-inch slice)
- 2 ounces coriander
- 2 ounces fennel seed
- 5 star anise
- 6 whole cloves
- 3-inch cinnamon stick
- 1½ tablespoons salt
- 4 tablespoons fish sauce
- 1 piece rock sugar (about 3 ounces)

**FOR THE BOWLS**

- 4 pounds divide by 8
- 1½ pounds beef eye round (thin slices)
- 1 medium yellow onion (thin slices)
- 3 or 4 green onion (use only green part, cut into thin rings)
- 1 cup chopped cilantro
- 2 teaspoon fish sauce (divide by 8)
- ½ pound raw eye of round, sirloin, London broil or tri-tip steak, thinly sliced across the grain (1/16 inch thick; freeze for 15 minutes to make it easier to slice)
- 1 medium yellow onion, sliced paper-thin, left to soak for 30 minutes in a bowl of cold water
- 3 or 4 scallions, green part only, cut into thin rings
- ⅓ cup chopped cilantro (ngo)
- Ground black pepper to taste

**FOR THE SIDE GARNISH**
- Basil, bean spout, chili and lime

## Instructions

Put coriander, fennel seed, star anise, cloves, and cinnamon stick into a cheesecloth bag. Set aside for the soup.

Prepare the bone: Place bones in minimum 12-quart capacity stockpot and cover with hot water. Over high heat, bring to boil. Boil vigorously two to three minutes to allow impurities to be released. Dump bones and water into sink and rinse bones with warm water.

As the same time in a large pot bring water to boil and returned the cleaned bone bring it to boil add ginger, shallot and dakon bring to boil over high heat, use ladle to skim any scum that rises to the surface, then lower flame to gently simmer for about two hours. Add beef chuck for one hour. Beef chuck meat should be slightly chewy but no tough. Remove it and place in bowl of ice cold water to 10 minutes (this prevents the meat from drying up and turning dark as it cools). Drain the meat; cool, then refrigerate. Allow broth to continue cooking; in total, the broth should simmer four hours.

One half-hour before serving put spice bags and continuous to cook for another half-hour.

Strain the pho broth through fine strainer. If desired, remove any bits of gelatinous tendon from bones to add to your pho bowl. Store tendon with cooked beef. Skim as much fat from the top of the pho broth as you like. Thinly slice cooked beef chuck roast.

Cook noodles: Fill five- or six-quart saucepan with water and bring to boil.

For each bowl, using 8-ounce rice noodle quickly in boiled water for 10-20 seconds, letting water drain back into saucepan and transfer to soup bowl. Add slice raw beef and sliced beef chuck roast, tendon. Garnish with onion, scallion and chopped cilantro. Finish with black pepper. And ladle in broth and served with the side garnish dish.

# Acknowledgments

From conception to publication, many people have helped this dream of mine come true, and I would like to thank these exceptional people to the moon and back.

Every book needs a great editor and a friend. *Pho for Life* has Wendy Toliver and I am forever grateful for the thoughtful editorial attention and suggestions that keep our voices one, our anthology extraordinary. Sincere appreciation, too, to Jen Baranick for help with the reading of the draft and offering valuable insights.

The creation of this anthology involved—and still involves—countless phone and email correspondences and continuous attention to spreadsheets, contracts, and the web-site. I wish to thank Quyen Ngo for her exceptional organizational and personal skills. Thanks also to Annie Kim Pham, for always being ready to help out at a moment's notice.

I am so grateful for Isabelle "Izzy" Kim, our book designer. Recently graduated from the Fashion Institute of Design & Merchandising, she brings with her not only creativity and the necessary skills, but also enthusiasm, dedication, and unwavering attention to detail.

Thanks to Peter Deltondo, Stork Digital, for building and securing our presence in the virtual community—ever so beautifully.

Special thanks to Michelle Krusiec for reminding us to give voice to our feelings, and for being such a great friend over the years.

I'm indebted to Phan Tran Hieu for his interest in my writing before I even realized the gift is within me.

Without Quinn Bui and Access Group Media, Inc., this book would not have been possible. When the going gets tough, Quinn reminds me that in every storm is a rainbow. Thanks also to Lorna Navales, the pillar that holds us artists together. These two are more than family to me.

And last but never least, all my gratefulness to three extra special ladies in my life: my lovely wife, Alice, and our wonderful daughters, Melody and Sabrina. They keep the tea pot hot and the light on for me, and it's always my honor and delight to have pho with them.

— *Mai Xuan Bui*

# About Michelle Krusiec

FILM, STAGE, TELEVISION ACTRESS AND WRITER MICHELLE Krusiec is best known for her starring role opposite Joan Chen in the romantic comedy *Saving Face*, directed by Alice Wu. The role gamered her critical acclaim and a Best Actress nomination in the 2005 Golden Horse Ceremony, Asia's equivalent to the Academy Award. Once described by the New York Post as "the Asian American Sandra Bullock," Michelle is known for surprising audiences with off-beat characters, intense emotional dexterity and chameleon like shifts that traverse both comedies and dramas.

Michelle originated the hit solo show *Made in Taiwan* which continues to four throughout the world today. For the most current information on Michelle's adventures, you can find her at www.michellekrusiec.com.

# About Wendy Toliver

AFTER GRADUATING FROM COLORADO STATE UNIVERSITY, Wendy Toliver was super excited to score a job at a hip and successful advertising agency in Salt Lake City, Utah. Only instead of in the creative department like she'd wanted, it was in the IT department. She struggled to become a computer nerd, and while she learned a lot about technology, she still longed to break into a more creative field. So she sat in on meetings held by the "creatives," gleaning enough to build a portfolio. In time, she began freelance copy writing for advertising agencies and publishers. She wrote several how-to and decorating books, followed by two books for Sterling's *Little Giant Encyclopedia* series. Then, after her first son was born, she had the crazy idea to write a novel. It started out as little more than an interesting new challenge, and she was surprised and delighted when Simon & Schuster offered her a publishing contract. Now the award-winning author of *The Secret Life of a Teenage Siren*, *Miss Match*, and *Lifted* and a mother of three boys, Wendy also makes time to volunteer, visit schools, coach soccer and basketball, wakeboard, and snowboard. She loves living in a small resort town in Utah, which provides plenty of inspiration for her future novels. Visit her online at www.wendytoliver.com.

# Credits